REALITY IN ACTION

How We Spend Our Time

Addressing Worry, Fear, Doubt, and Self-Blame

Jill Spiewak Eng

Crooked Circle Press®

Bailey, CO / 2026

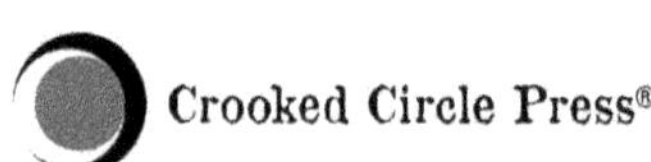

Author Photo by Willie McElroy.

ISBN: 979-8-9995552-5-0 (Paperback)
ISBN: 979-8-9995552-6-7 (EPUB)

Library of Congress Control Number: 2026931495

First Edition

www.crookedcirclepress.com

For Juniper

Contents

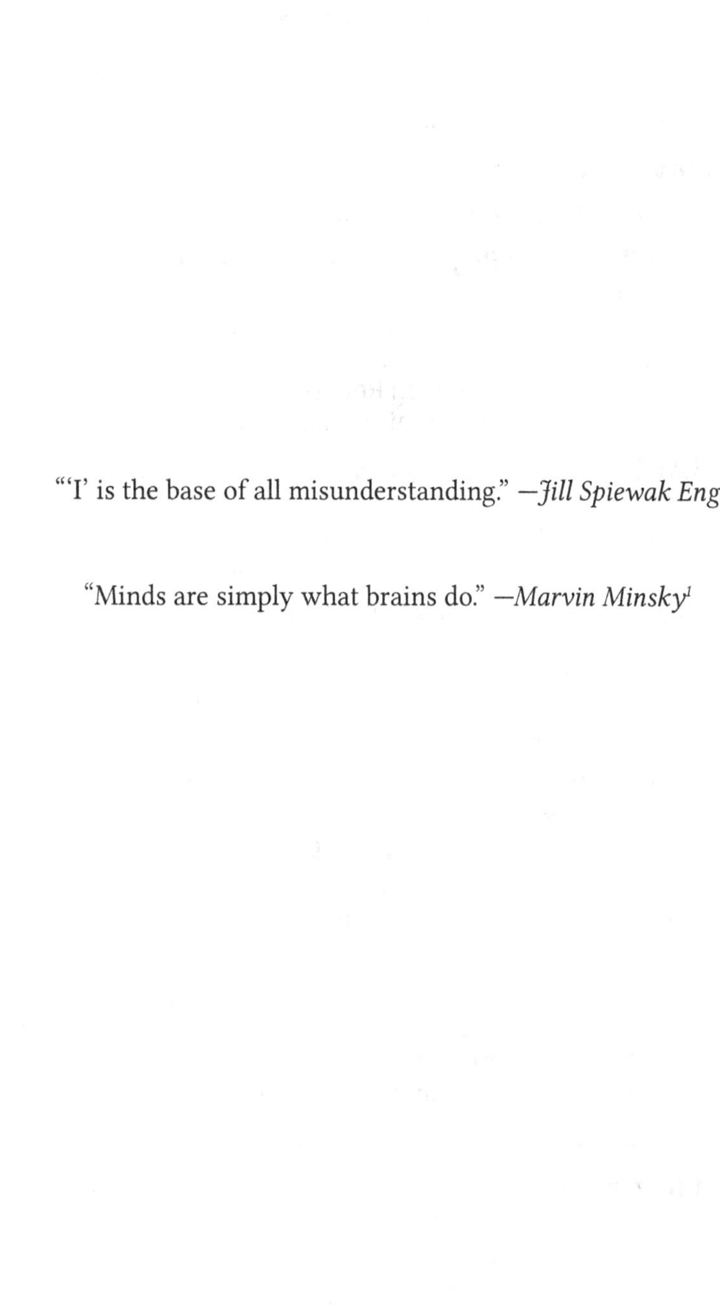

"'I' is the base of all misunderstanding." —*Jill Spiewak Eng*

"Minds are simply what brains do." —*Marvin Minsky*[1]

Preface

My first book, *Body Over Mind: A Mindful Reality Check*, was an assimilation of Eastern and Western awareness practices I had studied and taught over time. That information morphed into an original body of work I call *Mindful Reality*, which, among other things, expresses a firm statement that human behavior is physical and involuntary. My second book, *The Myth of Doing*, promoted a lens of nonduality, no-self, no free will, and hard determinism, referencing aspects of Western and Eastern philosophies, the Alexander Technique, psychology, cognitive science, neurophilosophy, and neuroscience. This third book, *Reality in Action: How We Spend Our Time,* expands those themes into intentionality, morality, moral responsibility, evolution, hard incompatibilism, luck, the criminal justice system, and the study of consciousness.

My work is the same throughout the books, which is a mindfulness/self-inquiry practice rooted in internalizing the awareness of the physicality and automaticity of behavior. My conclusion is that we are all correct in everything we do (despite the horrors), because anything else is physically impossible. Explaining what I call *involuntarism* is the heart of my attention. I take a purist view, canceling out concepts of voluntarism, a.k.a. conscious agency. The use of the words involuntary and voluntary is mine in the context of my writings. I encourage people to take from this material what they will, as we are all coming to a book like this from different backgrounds.

Introduction

The meat of this book points out what action is—from a material/physical standpoint—to counter and disqualify cognitive illusions that any of us can behave voluntarily. Real-time action is a body occupying space and moving in relation to its environment. I believe the misperception of action tricks us into mistaking our mental narratives for three-dimensional behavior. This propels us to pay attention to our thoughts and feelings rather than our bodily (skeletal) movements when seeking answers to how we should be living. I purport that this misapprehension grossly contributes to the illusions of self, free will, and consciousness.

The goal is to recognize involuntarism as the force of bodily movement that coordinates with the environment and flow of time—i.e., the automatic functioning of our organisms in conjunction with physical conditions around us, as Earth spins on its axis and revolves around the Sun. *Reality in Action* addresses my observations while referencing Western philosophers and educators, neurophilosophers, psychologists, cognitive scientists, evolutionary biologists, primatologists, and neuroscientists. Finally, I impart ways to realize involuntarism on a personal, macro level, offering accessible tools to counter inner judgments that imply we can act other than how we do. Compassion and acceptance are my interests for ourselves and each other.

Some Definitions

Free Will

> Free will has traditionally been conceived of as a kind of power to control one's choices and actions. When an agent exercises free will over her choices and actions, her choices and actions are up to her. But up to her in what sense? As should be clear from our historical survey, two common (and compatible) answers are: (i) up to her in the sense that she is able to choose otherwise, or at minimum that she is able not to choose or act as she does, and (ii) up to her in the sense that she is the source of her action. —*Stanford Encyclopedia of Philosophy: Free Will in Philosophy and Science*[2]

> The supposed power or capacity of humans to make decisions or perform actions independently of any prior event or state of the universe. Arguments for free will have been based on the subjective experience of freedom, on sentiments of guilt, on revealed religion, and on the common assumption of individual moral responsibility that underlies the concepts of law, reward, punishment, and incentive. —*Encyclopedia Britannica*[3]

Involuntary

1. done contrary to or without choice
2. compulsory
3. not subject to control of the will —*merriam-webster.com*[4]

Automatic

1. largely or wholly involuntary
2. acting or done spontaneously or unconsciously
3. done or produced as if by machine —*merriam-webster.com*[5]

Opening Statement

Involuntary Versus Voluntary

Regarding the word involuntary, I don't differentiate between reflexive behavior (like a knee jumping when tapped at the doctor's office, or a heart pumping) and actions such as kicking a ball or writing a letter. I put forth that different brain processes are behind various activities, while claiming that *every* move we make is involuntary, a.k.a. automatic, with no conscious choice/agent driving it. It is irrelevant to me whether or not there is an accompanying thought mirroring any behavior.

Sam Harris, a renowned philosopher, neuroscientist, and author, described the words voluntary and involuntary with regard to free will:

> There is a distinction between voluntary and involuntary actions, of course, but it does nothing to support the common idea of free will (nor does it depend upon it). A voluntary action is accompanied by the felt intention to carry it out, whereas an involuntary action isn't. Needless to say, this difference is reflected at the level of the brain. And what a person consciously intends to do says a lot about him. [...] But where intentions themselves come from, and what determines their character in every instance, remains perfectly mysterious in subjective terms. Our sense of free will results from a failure to appreciate this: We do not know what we intend to do until the intention itself arises. To understand this is to realize that we are not the authors of our thoughts and actions in the way that people generally suppose.[6]

Because my work looks at action simply on a skeletal level (ignoring accompanying intentions), I am set apart from the typical free will skeptic's view on the differentiation between voluntary and involuntary. Although our messages are the same in terms of acknowledging why we do not have free will—as Harris, for example, acknowledges that both thoughts and actions are automatic—my approach goes a step further. I argue against the consciously felt cause-and-effect link between thoughts and actions. For me, that disconnection flows from my assertion of what action is, i.e., the inherent status of a body's existence—"I am standing in the kitchen."

In a purist fashion, I deny the concept of voluntarism. As this book explains (as do my other two), conscious, voluntary action is an illusion, and instead, everything can be considered involuntary. This is because the human body is in a continual state of physical activity that precedes any observation/knowing of what that is; we find out what we do after the fact.

I understand that a knee jumping (in a reflex test) or an eye blinking seems different than taking a box of cereal off a supermarket shelf. Regardless, it is only descriptions and values that we assign to certain movements that mask their automaticity—in addition to the fact that some actions are tagged with intentional feels. But, if one pays close attention, they will notice that most of the time, there aren't intentional thoughts shadowing bodily movements. Rather, we customarily undergo muscle tension (that internally reads as voluntary assertion) and willful mind-chatter—which runs its silent mouth habitually. These each (and in tandem) relay false impressions of conscious agency.

CHAPTER I: The Physical Reality of Action

Regarding Action

Action is what we physically do in real time. More accurately, it is how we describe bodily movement, or collections of skeletal activity: "I am folding laundry," "I am editing the manuscript," "I am driving to the store." These motions are joint gestures. For some examples: a hand picks something up, a head turns toward a window, a finger sends an email, feet walk into another room, a jawbone moves and words come out, etc. If we are alive, our bodies are, by default, engaged in physical activities, and that is what I call action. Furthermore, because a human body continually occupies space, for each moment of its existence, it is in some specific positioning whereby no other simultaneous behavior is possible. This means it is physically impossible for any of us to do the things we (or others) believe we should, when/if we are not doing them.

We are regularly harassed by beliefs that there are things we should and should not be doing. These feelings consume us. A central component of this predicament is that we do not properly realize what action is; we misapprehend the word itself. Since this issue spans concerns from small to grave (from eating too much pizza to hurting another person), it is worth recognizing that underlying our common belief systems is an error of definition.

Action is what our bodies do, not what we think about doing. Although thinking is part of the organism's functioning, the information in its messaging is not tangible action, only an idea, prediction, or imagination of it. Inaccurately, we misperceive actions to be introspective deeds instead of skeletal articulations. This matter of doing lies at the heart of philosophy, law, science, politics, psychology, relationships, health, wealth, security, war, and everything we value, because we judge ourselves and each other based on what we believe we/everyone should and should not be doing.

I put forward that since human action is physical, i.e., real-time bodily movement, it is automatic/involuntary (I use these words interchangeably—see my Opening Statement). If we are alive, we are automatically/involuntarily doing something (in a describable act), even if that is only sleeping or lying down in a coma. Thus, it would be useful to consider the entirety of an individual's behavior from this standpoint. It may appear ridiculous to put eating into the same category as a murder; nevertheless, the same physical processes are behind the events—both are precipitated by unconscious neurological events.[7]

A consequence of automaticity is that a person must and can be only where their body is, doing what it is doing, no matter how undesirable the situation. Moreover, there is never an opportunity for one to consciously choose an action, since a body is always *already* in its state of activity before said person can notice what that is. This is because the rapid movement of the clock (as we track it) deems an observed action to be immediately something of the past, and moreover, consciousness arises too slowly to view an event in its present state.[8]

This all means we can never avoid how we act, because we (the perceived thinkers) have no opportunities to get behind the flows of our bodily movements the way it seems. I call this preclusion. The definition of *preclusion* is: "Something that prevents something or makes it impossible."[9] Specifically, some bodily placement and positioning is in process, which precludes another from occurring at the same time. Since it is impossible to move our bodies out of the way with what they are currently doing (because real-time life is exclusively *current*), everyone must be in whatever actions they find themselves in at all times.

Action in Action

> Unconscious neural events determine our thoughts and actions—and are themselves determined by prior causes of which we are subjectively unaware. — *Sam Harris*[10]

We can know of our own actions only once they have occurred, the same way we become aware of others' actions. Why do we believe we can know what our actions are going to be before we are in them? This is a trick of mind, though intuitive. Firstly, we've witnessed ourselves in prior circumstances that remind us of present events, and if something resembling A led to B in the past, we assume a similar outcome for the next time. Secondly, we hold beliefs that masquerade as knowledge about how we will act. Fundamentally, we assume there exist inner "selves" generating thoughts that are privy to the internal workings of our brains. This translates into the familiar thought/feeling/conviction: "I know what I am going to do," or, "She knows what she is going to do."

In addition to the fact that there is no (thought-driving) neural self in the human nervous system/brain,[11] how could a thought possess information about a future event that has never occurred? Thoughts that relay feelings, beliefs, emotions, judgments, intentions, ideas, opinions, intuitions, premonitions, etc., have no access to what precipitates nervous system outputs of behavior, nor to environmental influences. Furthermore, even from our subjective stances, we can see that thoughts present automatically; they emerge on their own (involuntarily), as we are suddenly aware of their messaging. Though it seems we choose thoughts and make decisions consciously through introspective powers, individuals would have to be in charge of their nervous systems to have that control. Who are those persons? Who is the thinker "I" we presume commands the choices of a brain that itself produces the feeling/thought "I"?

Regarding the apparent feelings that we consciously make decisions (and, subsequently, voluntarily/intentionally steer our actions), what mechanism are we assuming does that if not a self-based thought process? Isn't that where the sense of voluntary assertion seems to come from? If so, is it a thought that is responsible for an action? It feels like intentional thoughts spring up from a conscious, willful, self-source and then cause us to execute bodily movements. Neuroscience disproves this.[12] However, I argue that even without neuroscience, we can look closely at action to realize how choices materialize.

The human body (as a whole) is in a continuous state of (what we call) action. It is the actor/mover engaged in any activity. When we view a cat scratching, we say, "The cat is scratching." When we see a bird flying, we say, "The bird is flying." If we saw a puppy nursing, we would say, "The puppy is nursing." And, if we observed a woman driving, we would say, "The woman is driving." These are examples of actions, i.e., physical activities performed by bodies in real time.

Meanwhile, there are commonly thoughts bubbling up and dissolving in a human mind while a person is in their activities. Are these thoughts what cause people to carry out their actions? If so, would we assume the same for the cat, bird, and puppy? Thoughts are an integral, neurological component mentally projecting information that often correlates with the things we (humans) do, but they are not what make us be in our movements. Though they are part of the causal flow of what leads to specific behavior, they aren't the cause the way we perceive them to be.[13]

To support this point, it may be useful to consider that a body is *in* an action rather than doing an action. Doing implies a voluntaristic decision-maker, while being in an activity only requires the state of existence. When discussing a moon, for example, we would say it is *in* its action rather than doing its action because we do not attribute voluntary, conscious, decision-making power to a moon.[14] How do we draw the line between moons, planets, plants, bacteria, viruses, insects, fish, reptiles, other mammals, and ourselves, when evaluating motions of matter?

If one believes a thought precipitates an action—because it seems that way—when, then, is a choice deemed final (fully decided)? Since an individual can't know they will do something *until* they are aware their body is in that act, a decision only comes to fruition at the onset/completion of the gesture/task. No time before that can ensure the materialization of any consciously felt desire to act. (An example would be when you firmly decide to order Key Lime Pie for dessert. The waitperson arrives, and out of your mouth comes, "I'll have the German Chocolate Cake, please.") Moreover, thoughts, as producers of actions, could never be reliable, because they come and go randomly, on their own, offering no dependability. And finally, we do things all day long that we are barely aware of, and which aren't preceded by any type of thoughtfulness. Most of the time, we're simply in motion, or as the phrase goes, "going through the motions," with different kinds of thought processes erratically splashing around in the background.

Since evidence of a choice is limited to retrospect (we see what we did), it is the occurrence of action that marks a decision to do something. Anything prior to that is a guess. Though we may mentally plan activities, we can be affirmed of their actualizations only when demonstrated in real time, no differently than how we become aware of anyone/anything else's behavior.

Actions Are Physical

> Folk psychology is a name traditionally used to denote our everyday way of understanding, or rationalizing, intentional actions in mentalistic terms. [...] [This is also known] in the philosophical literature as commonsense psychology; naïve psychology; Homo sapiens psychology; the person theory of humans; the intentional stance; propositional attitude psychology; belief-desire psychology. —*Stanford Encyclopedia of Philosophy.*[15]

Paul Churchland, a philosopher and author who promotes eliminativist materialism, wrote this comment with regard to folk psychology, "[T]hat framework is a false and radically misleading conception of the causes of human behavior and the nature of our cognitive activity."[16]

When considering actions around us, we understand them to be physical events; we see or learn of people doing things. But, while there is never anything we personally do that isn't some kind of bodily movement, we tend to perceive our own actions as happening in our minds. We mistake thoughts for actions because that is how it feels (like an oozing or pushing out from our heads into the space). If we looked down at a sidewalk from a helicopter, we might see people walking—like viewing ants on the ground, we would encounter whole physical bodies in motion. If we watched an individual for a few blocks, we may notice how the person was walking, what they paused to look at, who they passed, if they stopped to fix their shoe, if they asked someone a question, etc.

However, with respect to our own persons moving through the days, we identify with our mental chatter. We associate our actions with our thought-filled narratives rather than our skeletal movements. Since introspection imbues the notion that we consciously generate thoughts, and that those thoughts, in turn, produce actions (putting us in charge of our behavior), we look to our inner monologues for meaning and solutions about how we should spend time, often overlooking what we do.

Why am I raising this point? Because absent thoughts *about* our activities (i.e., feelings, beliefs, ideas, emotions, intuitions, opinions, judgments—referred to as propositional attitudes and folk psychology),[17] there wouldn't be the same kind of self-judgment—only observation. Do other animals inwardly criticize or believe they know why they do things? We classify them differently. Is that because we have an ability to think and self-reflect? What does our sense of consciousness offer us in this vein? Do we know more about how and why we act (from our insides) than do lions, tigers, bears, or mosquitos?

Paul Churchland remarked in his book, *Matter and Consciousness*:

> [I]f none of the millions of other cognitive creatures on the planet are literally the subjects of propositional attitudes, what are we to say about the internal cognitive activities of humans? The same thing, argues the eliminativist. [...] [U]ltimately, he says, that linguaformal conception of our cognition is no more accurate for us than it is for any of the other creatures. Our brains work in essentially the same ways as all of our evolutionary brothers and sisters, and "propositional attitudes" have little or nothing

> to do with our mostly shared cognitive activities. If we want to really understand human cognition, he concludes, we need to get rid of our linguaformal self-delusion, and learn to discuss, and even to introspect, our cognition from within the conceptual framework of a theory (cognitive neurobiology) that is adequate to all of the Earth's creatures. Our current conception is useful, no doubt, but at bottom it must misrepresent our true cognitive economy.[18]

Our relentless focus on propositional attitudes muddles our awareness of our physical actions as they occur. Is there a difference between an interpretative account of our behavior and a chronicle of our activities? The former might consist of comparison, self-doubt, and self-beratement, while the latter would not. The former would be subjective, while the latter would be objective: "I feel like I shouldn't be eating this donut" versus "I am eating this donut." A simple report would mirror what is.

This brings me back to the question, "What are we calling action?" If actions are the continual, physical placements and strings of movement we find our bodies in (as opposed to our running commentaries about what we believe we should and should not be doing), there doesn't need to be confusion. Though our minds will self-critique, we don't need to look to them for guidance about how to live. As in a meditation, we can allow thoughts to come and go without getting on board emotionally in one direction or another. In the meantime, we can know actions do themselves (like other bodily functions we deem beyond our reach), because human organisms are automatically in streams of behavior just by existing. "I am standing in the living room, staring into space," is a direct description of an act. Without a projection of attitude onto this status, there is no evaluation of it as good, bad, right, or wrong. Brains, as organs, output behavior as kidneys do.

Unbiased observation, as relied on in science, is an efficient way to identify something that is physically taking place, like a waterfall. If we were studying birds, for example, we would indicate their motions from moment to moment, constructing causal explanations. Isn't that what wildlife experts do? They are clear and specific with their findings. Physicians do this when examining activity inside a body. A doctor doesn't describe an esophagus with a psychological portrayal of the tissue. Likewise, clinicians don't regard livers as immoral when they exhibit poorly. They remark on biological presentations in objective manners.

We can do this with our own beings when looking at how we spend time. We can consider action purely as physical movement, like we would events inside our bodies. If we don't personify or ethically blame organs, cells, and molecules, why do we do so with our so-called external (personal) behavior? Why are skin, eyes, and tongues considered separate from our material insides when they, too, are organs, cells, and molecules? Why don't we mentally register humans as exclusively physical? All organisms, as fully integrated, anatomical beings, act impartially because they are materially composed in their totalities. A human is as morally neutral in its outer manifestation as any internal display of its fleshy organization, since there is no identifiable demarcation between outside and inside.

The Difference Between Reality and Fantasy

Since actions are physical events in real time, we can look at them while we are in them (if we happen to be paying attention). We can see or feel (through touch) our bodies in relation to the surfaces beneath them. Because of gravity, we have ongoing, direct relationships with other material objects (couches, chairs, beds, floors) through dynamic transfers of weight. Any human walking on the ground is a physical happening like a boulder rolling down a hill, squirrel running up a tree, piece of seaweed swaying in the ocean, or horse galloping through a forest. All matter follows laws of nature based on its chemical makeup. How do we know things exist? We sense their material qualities. This is how we mark reality, including our own affairs.

Richard Dawkins, a prominent evolutionary biologist, elucidated in his book, *The Magic of Reality*:

> We come to know what is real, then, in one of three ways. We can detect it directly, using our five senses; or indirectly, using our senses aided by special instruments such as telescopes and microscopes; or even more indirectly, by creating models of what *might* be real and then testing those models to see whether they successfully predict things that we can see (or hear, etc.), with or without the aid of instruments. Ultimately, it always comes back to our senses, one way or another.[19]

To understand what action is, it helps to highlight the difference between fantasy and reality. Fantasy—imagination—presents as images, messages, or stories in our thought processes. Desirous feelings, as an example, are comprised of mental pictures/thoughts of things we wish to happen or not happen. Imagination is common as we envision ourselves in future scenes, though they may never occur. This is normal, but it can leave us less practiced in noticing what we do. Since there are discrepancies between real and fantasy-based goings-on, it is useful to note the distinction. This incongruity plagues all of us in one fashion or another and was the focus of my first two books. Though this book addresses the same awareness, it emphasizes that, as a global society, what we think of as action also rests largely in imagination.

It is my hope that by illuminating the physical and involuntary nature of human behavior, we can comprehend why it is impossible for anyone to not be engaged in the activities they are, no matter how disturbing. Since there isn't any individual who has the option to act other than how they do, reality always overrides fantasy (in terms of what is physically/causally necessary). This sheds light on the free will debate and the issue of moral responsibility, both of which sit at the hearts of criminal justice, education, work relations, government institutions, social and political lives, international relations, and so on. Acceptance of physical reality is valuable for all.

Physical Means Involuntary

Because human actions are physical, they are involuntary (automatic). Since existence and action are synonymous (one cannot be alive without being *in* some action: "I am lying on the couch"), we can first look at the state of existence to see how it is involuntary. The most obvious explanation is that coming into existence, i.e., being conceived (or born), emerges outside one's control. Furthermore, systems that maintain existence (respiratory, circulatory, pulmonary, endocrine, digestive, nervous system, etc.) run automatically; there is no conscious, willful self driving any of these, as with other organisms.

To exist means to be subject to physical laws, a primary one being gravity. Our bodies' weights (including our skulls—even when minds are lost in thought) are constantly being pulled toward Earth's center, leaving us naturally falling onto grounds, floors, or pieces of furniture. This phenomenon inherently puts us into continuous streams of action. I will explain. Because this gravitational dynamic mandates our bodies perpetually be in direct relationships with supporting surfaces, and those relationships intrinsically require verbs to describe them—"Jane is *standing* on the ground," "Ralph is *sitting* in the chair," "Molly is *reclining* on the couch"—existence alone qualifies as real-time action. Even without extra activity by a given individual—"Paula is *standing* on the bathroom floor *brushing* her hair"—action is a requisite condition of being human. (Regarding gravity, when not obviously sustained by surfaces, we still float in water or else sink to the bottom, can be suspended in air only with parachutes or cords, and must be attached to ropes and chains when engaging in serious rock climbing.)

Whether we are aware of our gravitational statuses or not, our bodies endure them full-time. While alive, physical laws mandate we can never disappear from space, time, or gravity, even when we space out, dissociate, or undergo an out-of-body experience. This explains why conscious, willful, voluntarism is unnecessary for us to be in our actions. If an organism exists, it is in some (describable) act, even if brain-dead.

CHAPTER II: How Things Happen

Intentions

Michael Gazzaniga, a leading expert in cognitive neuroscience, wrote:

> Our conscious lives depend on all kinds of automatic processes happening inside our brains. Though we can't even influence them by willed action, we continue to believe that we are in control of what we do.[20]

Additionally, Anil Seth, a neuroscientist and professor, spoke these words in his lecture, *Consciousness, Perception and Controlled Hallucinations*:

> Something most of us feel very central is the experience of intending to do things being the cause of things that happen; some people talk about this as free will.

In this presentation, Seth asked the audience members to clench their right fists and then to notice how it felt like the experience of intending to clench their fists caused it to happen. But he says that is not what happens at all. Instead,

> The experience of volition is the result and not the cause of that voluntary action. Experiences of volition, like any other experiences are best guesses. They're kinds of perceptions that help us explain particular combinations of data.[21]

People hold many opinions about how and why they (or others) end up where they do. Let us say Person X performed Action Y at Time Z. The first point I will make is that any action ever executed by a body is a *physical* act in real time, because there is no other kind. Some examples might include: Alice stole the jewelry, Mark hit his son, Rachel crashed into a tree, Roger ignited the bomb. At the time of occurrence, any of these doings was tantamount with the status of the individual's physical reality (their body was in that specific movement). Moreover, whether Person X was conscious of, or wanted to be in that act, they were in it.

A human body in motion is no different than a tornado (in this regard). It is a physical event/natural process taking place in time and space, since people in their existences/activities are molecular organizations driven by physical laws. The *presumed* difference between a theft and a tornado, for example, is that the former could have been prevented because it was delivered by a (thinking) person. Is the distinction that humans can be aware of themselves and tornadoes cannot? Or is it that we sometimes experience intentions before we do things?

The main reason people (and prosecutors) are interested in revealing intentions is to conclude that a person voluntarily caused their action and is, thus, properly guilty. Isn't that why we wouldn't morally blame a dog if it injured a baby, because it wouldn't have had a voluntary intention to do so? Or even if some would claim a dog had an intention, it would not have had control over that mental state? In the dog's case, we would view the incident as a demonstration of "positional" responsibility versus moral responsibility.

Philosopher and author Paul Breer described in his book, *The Spontaneous Self*:

> To say that I am positionally responsible for a given act means that, because the act arose here in this body/mind rather than somewhere else, I am liable for whatever the consequences may be of its arising. I am positionally responsible for my behavior, not because I am an agent who willed it to happen, but because I am the body/mind in which it arose. [...] Like all events in the natural world, that behavior has consequences; it serves as a stimulus to which other objects in the environment respond. Because I am the body/mind in which the behavior arose, I am

positionally liable for those consequences.[22]

If our dog attacks our baby, we may give it away to a place it could no longer harm someone, or even retrain it, but moral blame would be nonsensical. With humans, however, the firm assumption of a cause-and-effect link between intention and action (and/or the belief there is a self-agent behind the intention to begin with) convinces us the guilty party had an option to not have acted the way it did, or, in the least, to have not had the intention—if there was one. Do we view dogs differently because we perceive their behavior to be driven solely by nature? Why don't we consider human actions equally? The answer would likely be attributed to our intuitive confidence that thoughts guide and control bodily movement, and that people consciously (and freely) think up their thoughts.

Neuroscientist and author David Eagleman shared in his book, *Incognito*:

> [W]hen it comes to humans the legal system rests on the assumption that we do have free will—and we are judged based on this perceived freedom. However, given that our neural circuitry runs fundamentally the same algorithms as those of our pachyderm cousins, does this distinction between humans and animals make sense? Anatomically, our brains are made of all the same pieces and parts, with names like cortex, hypothalamus, reticular formation, fornix, septal nucleus, and so on. Differences in body plans and ecological niches slightly modify the connectivity patterns—but otherwise we find in our brains the same blueprints found in elephant brains. From an evolutionary point of view, the differences between mammalian brains exist only in the minute details. So where does this freedom of choice supposedly slip into the circuitry of humans?[23]

Renowned neuroscientist and primatologist Robert Sapolsky's point about intentions is that even if they were the cause of actions, the question that matters is, where do intentions come from?[24]

Similarly, Harris asks us to notice how our thoughts/intentions arise in consciousness out of nowhere, and how we cannot account for why we have the intentions we do.[25]

My emphasis is that conscious intentions do not cause actions. Though philosophers and scientists offer their reasons, my explanation is this: action is one and the same with existence (as explained in Chapter I: "Physical Means Involuntary"). And, because conscious, intentional thinking does not cause existence, it cannot cause action. Instead, human functioning is processed behind the scenes of introspection via automatic brain activity[26] influenced by whole-body coordination, environmental inputs, genetic factors, biological histories, and millions of other physical contributions.[27]

My first point, in the beginning of this section, was that any action ever referred to is a physical act in real time. My second point is to ask: How do we get from one act to another? Why do we suppose this transition requires a conscious, decision-making process? How is it possible it doesn't? Here is a way to look at it. The clock moves by itself—Earth rotates on its axis and revolves around the Sun—*without* our willful assistance. And, with this continual planetary movement, "now" is immediately "next," since we can't perceive the change (time progresses too quickly, from our perspective, to track one millisecond turning into another—apparent when using a stopwatch). The next second is already the new second, and so on, without any respite until our last breaths. Consequently, next happens to us, since there is no way to stop it from arriving, or to prevent ourselves from being in it. Accordingly (from the moments we are born until our deaths), our next actions are instantaneously upon us, without "our" being able to thwart or affect their contents.

Another way to capture this is that the only way we ever know of anything we are doing is because we see ourselves in the behavior. But it takes time for things we see to consciously register in our minds (when that even happens). By the times we are mentally aware of activities taking place by our bodies, they are of the past. Thomas Metzinger, philosopher and scientist specializing in the self-illusion, wrote about this time lag in his book, *The Ego Tunnel*, when discussing now-ness:

> And, of course, it is an illusion. As modern-day neuroscience tells us, we are never in touch with the present, because neural information-processing itself takes time. Signals take time to travel from your sensory organs along the multiple neuronal pathways in your body to your brain, and they take time to be processed and transformed into objects, scenes, and complex situations. So, strictly speaking, what you are experiencing as the present moment is actually the past.[28]

With regard to functioning, it is true that brains make decisions, but nonconsciously, because there are no conscious selves directing nervous systems the way it feels. Our decision-making mechanisms are mysterious to our "I"-centered minds. As a result, we discover our actions like we do weather conditions, i.e., after they are displayed to our senses.

I quote Gazzaniga from his book, *The Mind's Past*:

> By the time we think we know something—it is part of our conscious experience—the brain has already done its work. It is old news to the brain, but fresh to "us." Systems built into the brain do their work automatically and largely outside of our conscious awareness. [...] That most of the brain is engaged in activities outside conscious awareness should come as no surprise. This great zone of cerebral activity is where plans are made to speak, write, throw a baseball, or pick up a dish from the table. We are clueless about how all this works and gets affected. We don't plan or articulate these actions. We simply observe the output.
>
> This fact of brain-mind organization is as true for simple perceptual acts as it is for higher-order ac-

> tivities like spatial behavior, mathematics, and even language. The brain begins to cover for this "done deal" aspect of its functioning by creating in us the illusion that the events we are experiencing are happening in real time—not *before* our conscious experience of deciding to do something.[29]

The truth of whether one could have acted differently in any situation depends on how a body gets from point A to B. But, if our next actions are spontaneously upon us, we have no ways of influencing their prescriptions. Even when there are intentional thoughts in people's minds that correlate with executed acts, they are voluntarily powerless, since automatic brain processes produce the thoughts and the actions, as opposed to autonomous selves or conscious wills.

Additionally, there is no opportunity in one's personal timeline for a non-physical component (a soul, for example) to jump in and maneuver that body into a desired action, because, from start to finish, that organism is occupied with a stream of specific behavior. Lastly, the mere fact that we never have ways of knowing we will move into particular acts until we see that we did, is proof that humans, like all creatures, cannot consciously direct their behavior.

There is no way to alter this natural predicament. The reality of how actions emerge is starkly different from what our intuitions tell us. And, because thoughts present entirely on their own (like pulses in wrists), even when their messages align with behavior, their intentional content is not voluntarily relevant to the output of tasks. That would require a person (often referred to as an homunculus or ghost in the machine[30]) to reside inside a brain, drumming up thoughts, and that is not how nervous systems work. This fits in with Sapolsky's humorous description of, and frustration with, beliefs in free will. Note that because we are easily tricked by this illusion, it is possible to miss the absurdity in his language.

From his book, *Behave*:

There's the brain—neurons, synapses, neurotransmitters, receptors, brain-specific transcription factors, epigenetic effects, gene transpositions during neurogenesis. Aspects of brain function can be influenced by someone's pre-natal environment, genes, and hormones, whether their parents were authoritative or their culture egalitarian, whether they witnessed violence in childhood, when they had breakfast.

[...] And then, separate from that, in a concrete bunker tucked away in the brain, sits a little man (or woman, or agendered individual), a homunculus at a control panel. The homunculus is made of a mixture of nanochips, old vacuum tubes, crinkly ancient parchment, stalactites of your mother's admonishing voice, streaks of brimstone, rivets made out of gumption. In other words, not squishy biological brain yuck.

And the homunculus sits there controlling behavior. There are some things outside its purview—seizures blow the homunculus's fuses, requiring it to reboot the system and check for damaged files. Same with alcohol, Alzheimer's disease, a severed spinal cord, hypoglycemic shock.

There are domains where the homunculus and that brain biology stuff have worked out a détente—for example, biology is usually automatically regulating your respiration, unless you must take a deep breath before singing an aria, in which case the homunculus briefly overrides the automatic pilot.

But other than that, the homunculus makes decisions. Sure, it takes careful note of all the inputs and information from the brain, checks your hormone levels, skims the neurobiology journals, takes it all under advisement, and then, after reflecting and deliberating, decides what you do.[31]

As a side note, although Harris states that free will is illusory, he is vocal about the influence of beliefs on behavior.[32] He is especially known for his attitude that if religious ideas were reformed to scientific reason, people's actions would likely change. However, he fervently denies people can choose their beliefs, intentions, or actions.[33] He would also agree, that if, for example, a religious zealot mentally planned to engage in a terrorist attack, it wouldn't have been the thought that caused the pressing of a button.[34] Nor would there have been a *self* that generated the plan.[35] A human cannot consciously create their own wish, or voluntarily act *on* a desire, because there are no mechanisms for such pathways.

In sum, none of us can account for why we believe, or do, the things we do.[36] And when Sapolsky begs the question: "Where did the intention come from?" he answers with layers of antecedent biological events interacting with the environment, going back through evolution to the beginnings of the universe—all of which are beyond any person's control.[37] What I described above has also been termed, *The Illusion of Conscious Will*—that psychologist Daniel Wegner addressed in his such-titled book—which I referenced extensively in my book *The Myth of Doing*.[38]

Because I argue against a conscious connection between intentions and actions, my conclusion is that offenders, for example, don't have supernatural powers to know what they will do just because they (may) entertain interests in advance of their behaviors. More precisely, if intentions are unreliable tools in guaranteeing any of us the everyday results we want (otherwise we would successfully implement them all the time), how can they prove guilt after the fact?

Crime as Action

We assign moral responsibility to some behavior but not all. We do not feel morally responsible for the general functioning of our bodies, especially regarding issues we don't relate to. If a man gets lung cancer and never smoked, for example, he (most probably) feels no connection to the illness. If he had once been a heavy smoker, he may feel guilty.

If a young girl bursts out laughing in a classroom while another hiccups loudly, the former would most certainly be reprimanded or even shamed while the latter would be excused. If a driver at a stoplight doesn't see a pedestrian, accelerates when the light turns green, and hits the walker, this would be viewed differently than if they had seen the person coming, tried to make the light, and hit them. The former might be considered an accident while the latter a crime. Why? Because the driver's prior awareness of the walker makes us presume they could have driven differently.

These examples make sense to our notions of etiquette and morality but need to be examined further to understand how the events come about. Action (in my usage) is a specific, identified activity in real time: "Andrew is eating an ice cream cone," "Jenny is slicing a banana." Broken down, however, it is an uninterrupted stream of bodily movement that begins at the conception of an organism (spilling out of its ancestral biological history). Because of the ongoing physical course of cellular/molecular/atomic activity that is the life of a human being, it is impossible to point to the true origin/initiation of any physical act. There is always a movement preceding it.

Here are some other scenarios: A 39-year-old man is attending a public lecture. He thinks to himself, "I'm bored. I hate this; why does my wife make me come here? I should find a way to make this more interesting for myself." Then, he begins audibly uttering Batman voices from the movie he watched the previous night. Another example (let's call it Case 2) is a 47-year-old woman sitting quietly at the opera who is suddenly talking to herself aloud without having had any related thoughts or intentions beforehand. Would we have reason to assume that in Case 1 the man's thoughts were the cause of his vocal expression, and that he is guiltier (than the woman in Case 2) because he entertained prior feelings? If so, who is the self (inside him) that is guilty? Is it his thoughts? Is it the controller/owner of his thoughts? (Would that be his brain, nervous system, whole body, soul?) Did the man have any (conscious) control over his emotions of boredom or the outburst? If so, how?

In Case 2, without an intentional clue, the woman's pronouncements seem almost involuntary (even to herself), like a series of sneezes, though the behavior mirrors what we deem voluntary. She was sitting quietly, and then, suddenly talking. The words just came out of her mouth. Once she was aware of her state, she knew it was inappropriate (as did the man in Case 1), but what sparked the action? How are modes of self-control regulated? Even if one believes that thoughts cause actions, how can an action be purposeful when thoughts appear involuntarily to thinkers? What does purposeful, voluntary, or intentional mean?

I am not interested in culpability here, but rather, the spontaneity of thought and action. In Case 2, how was the woman's vocalization different than if she had sneezed? It was simply the next thing *she witnessed* her body doing in sequence with what it was doing immediately before. As noted earlier, with the clock's movement (which is constant and unstoppable), our next actions are displayed to us equally as to the people around us.

Let us now consider a graver situation. A person walks onto the street at night, sees someone sitting in a car, and shoots them. They may or may not have had a plan. There is no question they are *positionally* responsible[39] since the event came from their body, like a snake biting a child—and assumably pose a future threat to society because of the chance they will do it again. The question is, could they have prevented pulling the trigger? The answer is no, not if they pulled the trigger.

Understanding, biologically, how inappropriate and dangerous acts come about could lend value in determining penalties for crimes and alter dispositions toward fellow humans. Tragically, just because one must be removed from public life doesn't mean they had the option to have acted otherwise. This realization cannot directly reform the criminal justice system the way it implies (as we are learning no desirous/intentional thought can), but over time may change neurological patterning in brains in ways other knowledge has transformed social mores and laws.[40]

Without original/moral blame, what might a society look like? As Sapolsky repeatedly points out, we have already moved beyond blaming people for causing natural disasters (barring the way we view human involvement in climate change) and some diseases—after learning demonic/satanic possession, witchcraft, and bad parenting are not responsible for dangerous weather, epilepsy, and schizophrenia.[41] And most of us notice a mental shift when informed that aggressive, abusive behavior has resulted from someone's brain injury or tumor impairing a site of self-regulation.

Many naturalists work hard to cultivate a global community that would no longer justify criminal retribution, since they dispute just deserts (I define this in Chapter IV).[42] Some has been done in this direction, though progress is slow. It is, to say the least, challenging to convince people that humans do not possess free will, though in some circles, it is considered scientific fact.[43] Nonetheless, it is senseless to morally blame people for who they are or how they behave because no one creates themselves[44] or has the voluntary/conscious ability to manipulate the physical processes that cause their lifelong activity. As Tom Clark, founder and director of the Center for Naturalism, emphasizes, we are "fully-caused" creatures.[45]

Harris spoke to this issue in his book, *Free Will*:

> Viewing human beings as natural phenomena need not damage our system of criminal justice. If we could incarcerate earthquakes and hurricanes for their crimes, we would build prisons for them as well. We fight emerging epidemics—and even the occasional wild animal—without attributing free will to them. Clearly, we can respond intelligently to the threat posed by dangerous people without lying to ourselves about the ultimate origins of human behavior. We will still need a criminal justice system that attempts to accurately assess guilt and innocence along with the future risks that the guilty pose to society, but the logic to punishing people

will come undone—unless we find that punishment is an essential component of deterrence or rehabilitation.[46]

Free Won't

Free won't is a phrase that refers to changing one's mind in the form of consciously (freely) choosing to resist or override something one was going to do.[47] It originally came from neurophysiologist Benjamin Libet's attempt to show that even if an action had been initiated in a brain milliseconds before one was aware of an intention to act (which his experiments in 1983 revealed), there would still be an opportunity to veto the act, indicating that conscious control was not completely lost.[48] As an Alexander Technique teacher (a mind-body practice developed by F. M. Alexander in the 1920s), I am familiar with this scenario, since the crux of that work educates people how to decidedly employ conscious control over unwanted habits. It is experienced as a pause or voluntary redirection of an undesired action. (In his time, his discoveries were considered revolutionary among philosophers/authors John Dewey and Aldous Huxley—the former of whom endorsed it as an example of free will.)

However, this veto, or any mental invocation of free won't, is still a kind of thought process. Free will and free won't equally refer to a misconception that we make actions happen through introspective powers—whatever their nature. But there are no conscious "I's" privy to neurological causes since there are no selves at helms of nervous systems. Though the feeling of free won't can be a significant experience, it too is a result of automatic brain processing. In the same way one alcoholic stops drinking while another doesn't, we can't say the former gave it up *because of* their desire—or that they caused their intention. They were lucky their behavior changed, while the latter was not. There is no way to know why some people are so fortunate as to change habits.

Familiar feelings of conscious voluntarism make us assume interests and purposeful thoughts directly affect actions. Regardless, neuronal operations influenced by neurotransmitters, hormones, past experiences, environmental effects, genes, ancestry, and evolution—for some examples—are responsible for moving our bodies into their specific activities.[49] Free won't is a fancy term for free will, but neither can be the truth of the matter.

CHAPTER III: Consciousness/Illusionism

The Word Consciousness

Psychologist and author Jeffrey Mishlove interviewed legendary cognitive and computer scientist Marvin Minsky about his book *Mind as Society*:

> Minsky: "[W]hat I suggest in this book, and the kind of theory I work on, is that the mind is many hundreds of different kinds of computers. It took us four hundred million years to evolve from the time that we were fish to humans, and what happened in that time isn't that the brain just got bigger, but it got more complicated[.]"
>
> Mishlove: "Well, many people would say, by definition, if it's a machine it's not conscious."
>
> Minsky: "Well, I think that's a funny way to use words, and that's absolutely right. I hear this all the time. But then, if you ask people, 'Well, what do you mean by consciousness?' they say mysterious things. I think we can explain consciousness the way science explains other things. You work for a while, and you try to say what is it that we're really talking about—what are the phenomena, what happens in consciousness that I have to explain? And if you talk to most people, they have a very fuzzy idea of consciousness. They say, 'It's being aware of everything that's going on.' Well, we're not. 'It's knowing what your mind is doing.' Well, we don't. When I talk, I haven't the slightest idea of the processes that produce the words. So how I make the words is not conscious, and when you talk to me, and these sounds come in and I make sense of them, yes, I'm conscious of the words in a sense, but I'm not at all conscious of the tremendously complicated process-

> es. We ought to have more respect for ourselves, and the joke—I think—is that when a person says, 'I'm not a machine,' they're showing a lack of respect for people."[50]

The global definition of consciousness is unclear. Why the concern about the word? Firstly, it puts resources toward scientific exploration if believed a certain way. Secondly, it sets the groundwork for treatment of other organisms wrapped around who/what suffers from pain. Thirdly, it ties in with a mistaken belief in free will. This instills blame toward ourselves and others that leads to mental health, social, political, economic, legal, and healthcare stigmas, inequalities, and retributive policies.

What many call consciousness is a creed in a "selfy"[51] engagement in thinking, perceiving, experiencing, and trying, with a sense of being able to control one's circumstances. Additionally, there is a wide range of pseudoscience packaged in theories such as manifestation, energy work, collective consciousness, law of attraction, paranormal experience, premonition, witchcraft, telekinesis, telepathy, channeling, and distortions of quantum mechanics, to name a few. A trendy word for these is "woo."

Pertaining to the worlds of Western philosophy of mind, science of mind, and neurophilosophy, I agree with a minority of others who argue that no one is conscious the way it feels. I am considered an illusionist in this regard. Most illusionists claim consciousness exists but is not what it seems. I concur. One might ask: to whom is that seeming occurring, or who is undergoing the illusion? I would answer: no one. Instead, brains produce representations of illusory selves possessing selfhood, subjectivity, a point of view, experience, personal control, and anything else people mean by the word consciousness.[52]

Commonly, there is a belief in an extra layer of something, often referred to as consciousness—either physical or nonphysical—needed for us to make choices the way we do. But, there is no middleman for this to occur, as there isn't with other species making the decisions they do.[53] Rather, nervous systems are information processors—without central commanders[54]—outputting behavior in all organisms that house them.[55] Ours happens to include (human types of) spoken, written, and thinking languages that evolved from prior evolutionary states. Many creatures go to spots in forests, see their prey, and attack. Though some humans do that, we also make grocery lists, drive to markets, and purchase food. For some reason, we are misled to believe our brands of action necessitate conscious qualities above and beyond physical functioning.

Paul Churchland eloquently asserted:

> [T]he important point about the standard evolutionary story is that the human species and all of its features are the wholly physical outcome of a wholly physical process. Like all but the simplest of organisms, we have a nervous system. And for the same reason: a nervous system permits the discriminating guidance of behavior. But a nervous system is just an active matrix of cells, and a cell is just an active matrix of molecules. We are notable only in that our nervous system is more complex and powerful than those of our evolutionary brothers and sisters. Our inner nature differs from that of simpler creatures in degree, but not in kind.[56]

Before entering the next section, I would like to highlight the influence of René Descartes (an early 17th-century philosopher, scientist, and mathematician) on modern-day beliefs. He famously pronounced the mind to be independent of the physical organism. He was not the first, but his dogma has remained intuitive—for the average person—of a separation between the material body and an immaterial mind/soul.[57] People have different ideas about what this is, but all these centuries later, philosophers and scientists throw around terms like Cartesian dualist and Cartesian materialist to label those who infer something mysterious about subjectivity and experience.

Paul Churchland described Descartes' substance dualism:

> Descartes theorized that reality divides into two ba-

> sic kinds of substance. The first is ordinary physical matter, and the essential feature of this kind of substance was said to be that it is *extended in space*: any instance of it has length, breadth, and height, and occupies a determinate position in space.
>
> [...] But there was one isolated corner of reality he thought could not be accounted for in terms of the mechanics of matter: the conscious reason of humankind. This was his motive for proposing a second and radically different kind of substance, [...] a substance whose essential feature is the activity of *thinking*. [...] This view is known as *Cartesian dualism*.[58]

Is Consciousness a Hard Problem?

Consciousness, in Western philosophical and neurophilosophical discourse, is broken down into phenomenal consciousness (phenomenality, subjectivity) and access consciousness ("availability for use in thinking or guiding action and speech"[59]). From here on, when I use the word consciousness, I will mean phenomenal consciousness. A central word in this discussion is qualia (the singular noun is quale), which refer to "the introspectively accessible, phenomenal aspects of our mental lives."[60] Prominent psychologist and writer in consciousness studies, Susan Blackmore, defined qualia as "The ineffable subjective qualities of experience, such as the redness of red or the indescribable smell of turpentine."[61]

There are two well-known philosophers behind this topic: Thomas Nagel and David Chalmers. In 1974, Nagel formalized a definition of consciousness by raising the question, "What is it like to be a bat?"—inferring there is something it is *like* to be something/someone (in our case, *each* of us).[62] He concluded that if there is something it is like to be that organism, something it is like *for* that organism, then *it* is conscious. Followers of this trend are called *mysterians*.[63] They claim consciousness will never be explainable by science, because it regards private experiences, which they declare science cannot test.[64]

The phrase "the hard problem of consciousness" was coined in 1994 by David Chalmers, who wanted to distinguish what he called subjectivity/experience from easy problems that, *in principle*, science knows how to solve.[65] "They include perception, learning, attention, and memory; how we discriminate objects or react to stimuli; how being asleep differs from being awake."[66] The hard problem—on the other hand—asks: how can objective brains with their billions of neurons produce private experiences?[67]

There are various responses to Chalmers' perspective. Some concur there is a hard problem; Harris is vocal in that camp, and I address him later in this chapter.[68] Others believe there isn't a hard problem, stating that there is a way for science to find neural correlates of consciousness in the brain—and they go hunting for those through research.[69] As mentioned above, I fall into the category of illusionism, which purports there to be no hard problem, since consciousness is an illusion—that is, not what it seems. I align with other illusionists who say easy problems can address (phenomenal) consciousness. This is different than those hunting for neural correlates of consciousness, but I do not delve into that here. If you are interested in the range of approaches, Blackmore wrote a wonderful book called *Consciousness: A Very Short Introduction.*

In that book, she shared her perspective:

> [C]onsciousness might be intrinsic to complex biological processes and inseparable from them. [...] In this case there is no need to ask why consciousness evolved, because any creature that evolved with intelligence, perception, memory, and emotions would necessarily be conscious as well. There is no added extra and no sense in talking about "consciousness itself" or "ineffable qualia". Thinking about consciousness this way, there is no deep mystery and no hard problem. What we need to do is explain why

> there *seems* to be a hard problem and why we *seem* to be having ineffable, non-physical, conscious experiences. In other words, consciousness is an illusion because neither consciousness nor the hard problem are what they seem to be. So the task is to explain how the illusions come about.[70]

She concluded:

> We do not need to explain how consciousness is produced by, or emerges from, the objective activity of the brain, because it does not. We do not have to explain the magic difference between brain activity which is conscious and that which is not, because there is no difference. We do not have to wonder how subjective experiences evolved and whether they have a function of their own, because they do not. There is no stream of experiences—only fleeting events that give rise to a false impression.[71]

This is how Blackmore sees the illusion appearing: she suggests people ask themselves, "Are you conscious now?" or "What were you conscious of a minute ago?" Her research reveals this is an almost impossible question to answer, since people's responses are unclear and nonspecific. She deduces that we assume we know what the word is referring to, but when asked directly, that presumption is mistaken. Or, as she remarks, it's only when asked the question, "Are you conscious now?" that people suddenly feel conscious. Otherwise, how could you know you were conscious before being asked?[72]

Daniel Dennett and Keith Frankish are leading illusionists in consciousness studies. Dennett was a renowned philosopher, cognitive scientist, and author who recently passed—I reference him later in this chapter. Frankish, a prolific philosopher and writer, has compared phenomenal consciousness to a rainbow:

> Consciousness is as real as a rainbow. It exists, but it is not a private qualia world, any more than a rain-

> bow is a physical arc in the sky. So trying to find the neural correlates of the qualia world is as sensible as trying to find an arc-shaped structure in the atmosphere after a rain shower. And searching for a solution to the Hard Problem is like looking for the pot of gold at the end of a rainbow![73]

Philosopher and author Alex Rosenberg is in a similar camp. He has argued that subjective points of view and subjective experiences are illusory, stating they can be accounted for by easy problems:

> So, why suppose there is a problem lurking in Nagel's question about what it's like to be a bat? Pretty clearly, the problem is the result of taking introspection seriously. It's the feeling introspection gives us that even after everything about the brain is known, there will still be something left unexplained. Why? Because introspection can't conceive how causes, effects, and composition explain what experience is like. But there is no reason to allow introspection to guide us.[74]

Here is my attempt at explaining the illusion of consciousness. I propose that we have built-in misperceptions of our physical realities, i.e., what we and our actions *are*. I claim this is a result of our habitual fight-or-flight statuses (chronic muscular reactivity to everything we do) that stimulate thought patterns projecting illusions of conscious selfhood and control. (This is an awareness related to the Alexander Technique.) This combination of muscle tension and thought relays an impression of what I call *voluntarism*. This bolsters intuitive, introspective assumptions of experiencing selves that *have* emotions, desires, beliefs, feelings, ideas, goals, and opinions, and that *use* them to produce corresponding actions. The presumption of free will and many of the ways people use the word consciousness are webbed into this projection.

The fight-or-flight contraction of reactive muscle tension

(also referred to as startle reflex) that is familiar to us—though we're generally unaware we're in it unless pointed out—can be released temporarily and repeatedly. When done so (especially around muscles and bones in the skull/face, neck/throat, spine/chest, hands, and feet), thoughts momentarily disappear. No glimpses of conscious selves remain, and feelings of owning/having experiences evaporate. In my opinion, this cancels out the existence of a stream of consciousness (a term coined by psychologist William James),[75] and aligns with Blackmore's question exercise—"Am I conscious now?"— that also denies a stream.[76] It also speaks to her opinion about why we shouldn't be hunting for neural correlates of consciousness, but rather correlates of *processes* that create the illusions and make them disappear.[77]

Here is my argument against a hard problem of consciousness. There is a glitch in Nagel's phrasing of what it's like to be a bat, because it implies a some*one* to be like. But there are no "yous" or "I's" for whom it is like anything to be—even for humans—since neuroscience discloses there are no selves in brains.[78] There are only illusions of subjectivity and voluntarism that come and go, causing confusion.

In his book, *The Atheist's Guide to Reality*, Rosenberg illuminated:

> If there were a subjective point of view that belongs to the self, then this would indeed be a fact not fixed by the physical facts. Since the physical facts do fix all the facts, there is no such point of view, no self, no person, no soul. That is the last illusion of introspection.[79]

Scientifically speaking, we need a different approach that explains the *feelings* of what we mean by consciousness that imply selves, subjective experiences, qualia, free will, conscious will, volition, voluntarism, etc., and what those come from. Then, the word consciousness can be toned down to mean states like awareness, perception, thought, emotion, attention, or awakeness—qualities accounted for by easy problems—losing its hyper-importance and separation from basic functioning.

The Self in Our Head

Philosopher and author Bruce Hood, from his book, *The Self Illusion*:

> We all know the power of visual illusions to trick the mind into perceiving things incorrectly, but the most powerful illusion is the sense that we exist inside our heads as an integrated, coherent individual or self. As a self, we feel that we occupy our bodies. On an intellectual level, most of us understand that we need our brains, but few of us think that everything that makes us who we are can be reduced down to a lump of tissue.[80]

In addition to the mirage that we can access inner selves via focusing on our thought processes, this preoccupation leaves us ignoring our real-time behavior. It directs attention toward our imaginations rather than our bodies in the spaces they occupy. This resembles the seduction of a magic trick, where we are blind to the actions behind the presented fantasy because the illusion is hypnotizing.[81] But, unlike a magic trick, our bodily movements—which are our real actions—are always accessible for us to discover.

I allege it is our habitual, muscular, fight-or-flight reactivity that establishes this illusory condition, because it puts organisms into distracted thinking (which emits strongly felt bouts of not-hereness). Mind-wandering[82] renders our awareness of our physicality almost non-existent, as if we disappear from time and space (or come and go). Chronically, we perceive our bodies to be where our thought stories are: at the supermarket, for example, when we are standing in our kitchen.

Like with optical illusions, where it is impossible to simultaneously view two images embedded in one drawing (such as the famous sketch portraying the front of a woman's face or her profile, a Necker cube, or the duck/rabbit image), we cannot observe our bodies in their activities *while* focusing on our mental narratives. This is because sensory perception and introspection are mutually exclusive. We flicker back and forth, generally identifying more with the scenes in our minds.

Meanwhile, we are lured by our inner movies into believing *they* represent our lives, while our real-life happenings take place by our bodies in their physical environments, moment-to-moment. One is fantasy; the other, we can touch and see visually. There is a graphic I enjoy of what appears to be a large white triangle surrounded by black shapes and lines. But, when viewed carefully, we realize the *only* marks on the page are the black ones, while the negative space creates an optical trick of a white triangle. This is similar to our physical lives being *overlooked* by our narratives: One feels real; the other doesn't. One is real; the other isn't. (To clarify: the messaging output from the brain—our inner narrative—is real; however, its story is often not a true reflection of our physical actions.)

While lost in thought, we are at best left with fragmented senses of our structural bodies, not recognizing we are physical wholes, continually occupying space, and by default, always in identifiable acts. Awareness of our corporeal existences and spatial whereabouts is glazed over by heads in clouds. This is normal. I point it out only to highlight that what we frequently believe about our lives are at best guesses. Rather, seeing our continuous skeletal activities (or sensing them through touch and weight)—including words exiting mouths and fingers—provides honest, grounded accounts.

The sense of not-hereness (dissociation) is specifically due to the chronic muscular tension around the skull-spine juncture (Atlanto-Occipital or A-O joint)—which is a condition that develops as we move beyond childhood.[83] It leaves an impression that our heads are not permanently attached to our spines (and the rest of us)—as if they (*we*) could leave the whole to attend to our needs out in the world. Remarkably, when this joint is released into its natural dynamic state (a practice learned in the Alexander Technique), a feeling of hereness is restored. But, even when one achieves that balance temporarily, muscle tension, with its corresponding mind-wandering, soon clicks back into its habitual default mode.

In essence, this stiffened, compromised status of the head/neck joint spins an internal, psychological creed of a *separate* self from the physical organism, resonating as a mind-body split (duality). Since we erroneously believe *we* are selves residing in our minds/brains, it makes sense that this tension pattern—that relays a seeming of our heads being *split off* from our spines—would read as our *persons* being disconnected from our bodies in their immediate environments, a.k.a., *here*. This delusionary detachment, or separateness, of a cerebral (mental) self from our other anatomical parts, aligns with Descartes' dualism in his claim that the *thinking* part was a soul, i.e., a non-physical entity.

I also have curiosity about the confluence of that tension pattern congealing when we begin identifying as selves in language—both starting to occur strongly between the ages of two and four. To note, if the inner story of "me" disappears when the (A-O) joint is released, it seems likely the two go hand in hand (the reactive muscle tension and the mental dissociation resulting from identifying as an inner self). Alexander called the entirety of this phenomenon "habit." This issue is unavoidable in humans; however, it may shed light on our innate senses of, and relatability to, concepts of selfhood and subjectivity that feel undeniable.

In truth, the mind is a word representing nervous system processes that have emerged via evolution and natural selection,[84] and its machinations are unquestionably part of the material human being. There is no mind-body split because there is only the whole organism carrying out its systematic functions in coordination with its environment.

The Story of a Voluntary Self

> But the strangest and most wonderful constructions in the whole animal world are the amazing, intricate constructions made by the primate, *Homo sapiens*. Each normal individual of this species makes a *self*.

> Out of its brain it spins a web of words and deeds, and, like the other creatures, it doesn't have to know what it's doing; it just does it. —*Daniel Dennett*[85]

Although we only find out about our actions after the fact (when we see ourselves engaged in them), we hold convictions that there are conscious "I's" in our minds/brains acting on our behalves and knowing ahead of time what our bodies will do. Both these beliefs are part of the illusions of selves, free will, and consciousness. When Dennett remarked above, referring to us, "Out of its brain it spins a web of words and deeds, and, like the other creatures, it doesn't have to know what it's doing; it just does it," he meant that those brain outputs (the "words and deeds") are automatic rather than consciously executed.

I address the collective illusion of a self, free will, and consciousness, by pointing out that humans are naturally in their thoughts and actions by simply existing. This disqualifies the necessity of an extra ingredient (consciousness) to make us do what we do, regardless of how sophisticated acts may seem. It is a misperception that we *cause* our thoughts and behaviors through conscious, voluntary, self-forces. Although thoughts can feel willful, invoking notions there are inner selves consciously (voluntarily) generating them—and our actions—the source of all thinking and other activity is invisible to our awarenesses. What we feel, in these instances, is extraneous muscle tension tricking us into believing that there is something else going on.

As already stated, many of these illusions stem from a misapprehension of what actions are. They are neither thoughts nor muscle tension (the familiar sensations we call effort) and are not precipitated by voluntaristic pushes of selves or wills. Actions are *descriptions* of bodies' placements and positionings. "Laura is putting on her shoes," "Andy is feeding the dog." Time marches, undetectably, presenting our actions to us through flashes of sight, sound, touch, etc.—like weather conditions.

Muscle reactivity intuitively reads as self-caused trying, doing, exertion, control, causation, and power. Subsequently, we misunderstand *it* to be action. We wrongly identify with the muscular sensation (without realizing) and presume our behavior to be coming from a conscious self that is an all-in-one fountain of voluntary thinking, decision-making, and bodily motion. Conversely, we can't *feel* action, since it is the activity of neurons signaling muscles to move bones into gestures and tasks—in the same way we don't claim ownership of blood circulation, gut microbe production, liver filtration, or hormone secretion. Neuromuscular skeletal movements (a.k.a. gestures, tasks, actions)—including words coming out of fingers and mouths—are automatic, *like those other involuntary systems.* But the tension on top registers as willfulness coming from a self inside. That is what I call the illusion of voluntarism. We mistake molecular activity to be agent-behavior.

When Blackmore suggested putting resources toward finding neural correlates that explain the illusion of consciousness—and what makes it appear and disappear[86]—this is the type of thing to look at. I say this because when we momentarily come out of fight-or-flight, especially in the vicinity of the (back of the) head-spine connection, there is no sensation of a self, or to be *like* anything—as in Nagel's premise. In the absence of being like anything, there is no subjective experience to consider.

Experience/Experiencer

Metzinger wrote:

> In ordinary states of consciousness, there is always someone *having* the experience—someone consciously experiencing himself as directed toward the world, as a self in the act of attending, knowing, desiring, willing, and acting. There are two major reasons for this. First, we possess an integrated inner image of ourselves that is firmly anchored in our feelings and bodily sensations; the world-simulation created by our brains includes the experience of a *point of view.* Second, we are unable to experience and introspectively recognize our self-models *as* models; much of the self-model is, as philosophers

might say, *transparent.* Transparency simply means that we are unaware of the medium through which information reaches us. We do not see the window but only the bird flying by. We do not see neurons firing away in our brain but only what they represent for us.[87]

Throughout this section, I reference Harris. Although I appreciate his work regarding free will, atheism, and mindfulness, I differ with his opinion on consciousness. He aligns most closely with Nagel's *mysterianism* (that consciousness is "the fact of subjectivity") and Chalmers' assertion of a hard problem, as well as with psychologist Steven Pinker and philosopher Colin McGinn, who suggest consciousness is something we will never be able to understand.[88] Though he is not alone in his attitude, I use his work as an example.

As a strong proponent of calling the self an illusion,[89] Harris professes we can have consciousness without a self because, he has written, "Consciousness is prior to it, a mere witness of it, and, therefore, free of it in principle."[90] He purported, "Only consciousness can know itself—and directly, through first-person experience."[91] When he says that, it seems he is implying an experiencer, just that the experiencer is somehow not a self. My question is: What is that first-person he is referring to if not a felt self? There cannot be a first person, or subjectivity, if there is no self, because a first person implies a subject. I stand with others who assert there is no difference between a self, first-person, first-person point of view, subjectivity, subjective experience, or consciousness (as in what it is like to be a bat).[92]

Although Harris' stance is largely influenced by his Buddhist meditation practice,[93] being someone versed in similar education, I disagree with his interpretation. In meditation, it is possible to introspectively observe the emergence and dissolution of thoughts (in the background of whatever mantra is being used: the breath, a sound, etc.). In this case, Harris and others claim it is consciousness that becomes aware of the inner stream of the thinker "I"/ego/self. However, this is tricky, because even though there is a sense of a watcher (sometimes referred to as the Self or Awareness), the question is, what/who is that?

While I understand the assignment of such vocabulary—Consciousness, Awareness, or Self—it is the brain that creates all the (mental) representations.[94] Thus, I do not endorse that the ability to watch thoughts—in a meditation or self-inquiry practice—is a state to be called consciousness (especially with a capital C). While I acknowledge it is meant to imply nonduality (the absence of a separate self emanating from a thinker "I"/ego), I find the word consciousness confuses things by indicating another layer that also doesn't exist (and still reads as dualism). Nothing is looking at, or is, the mind. Identification with any experience (even the supposed consciousness) is part of the illusion of self and its extended subjectivity. This is accounted for in what Dennett calls the Cartesian theater.

In a wonderful video called *The Magic of Consciousness*, Dennett stated, "The Cartesian theater is my derisive negative term for the imaginary place in the brain where an inner witness sits, the audience sits, and enjoys the show of consciousness."[95] He explained that what is wrong with this is there is no conscious observer (homunculus) sitting in the theater looking at the screen, and that there is no place in your brain where it all comes together for consciousness. Dennett emphasized that empirically, we know this does not exist, arguing that, in reality, it's all machinery without a supervisor, watchman, or boss. He called this, the dilemma of the subject. He expressed that if you leave the subject in your theory of consciousness, i.e., "I"/ego, you cannot really be explaining consciousness, while people like Chalmers claim that if you don't leave the subject in the theory of consciousness, you're evading the hard problem—a.k.a. experience/subjectivity. Dennett stressed that we must get rid of the idea of the subject altogether.

Meditation can still be valued as a mental exercise that can put one into a transcendent state beyond habitual mind chatter. This is a wonderfully powerful tool. It is a cognitive skill that changes the perception of our usual self-talk, leaving us with a different type of attention that also results from neuronal functioning—not something outside the processes of the brain. Being someone who adores meditation, I believe we can enjoy detecting the prevalence of thoughts—versus being lost in thought—without labeling the practice with a magical, mystical word.

Harris specifically uses the phrase "contents of consciousness," and is well known for his expression that thoughts appear *in* consciousness.[96] In my opinion, the indication of contents (streams, or qualia) requires selves to classify them. What else do we mean when we feel like we have or are a self? Isn't it the force or source *behind* the feeling or introspective seeing of our (so-called) experiences?

Metzinger summarized:

> It has now become clear that we will never solve the philosophical puzzle of consciousness—that is, how it can arise in the brain, which is a purely physical object—if we don't come to terms with this simple proposition: that to the best of our current knowledge there is no thing, no indivisible entity, that is *us*, neither in the brain nor in some metaphysical realm beyond this world. So when we speak of conscious experience as a *subjective* phenomenon, what is the entity *having* these experiences?[97]

I do not believe there is any kind of content of consciousness we can acknowledge that doesn't come through as information received by an inner knower, seer, or experiencer. In other words, the appearance of messaging that invokes us to say we're having an experience—whether by a self or consciousness—is equally illusory. I get how subtle this is. Ultimately, I see no difference between the subjective someone (of Nagel's what it's like to be a bat and Chalmers' hard problem—a.k.a. consciousness) and a self. Rather, they reflect different types of perception, awareness, and attention.

For example, if a person is listening to music and relays having an experience from that music, the only way they know of that is because of a presentation of language/imagery in their thought process. In some fashion, the experience is referred to as such a thing. And what is believed to be holding/having that descriptive thought process if not a perceived self with a unique, subjective point of view? The apparent acknowledger of the luscious experience resulting from ears being exposed to artistic sound waves is a version of an illusory self.

Consequently, I call any messaging in a so-called mind "thought," regardless of its *experiential* nature. In my view, the seeming of or identification with the word consciousness is still a type of thought process. This is because awareness of anything turns into thought the instant it is perceived as some*thing*, i.e., labeled.

In his book, *Waking Up*, Harris used the phrase "the lights are on,"[98] which emboldens the idea of consciousness as something beyond perception, sight, hearing, attention, etc. How is the lights being on different from sensory information-processing of nervous systems (an easy problem)? Why the extra term consciousness as a force of function? I appreciate Dennett's take on this:

> Notice that it presupposes something we have worked hard to escape: the assumption that consciousness is a special all-or-nothing property that sunders the universe into two vastly different categories: the things that have it (the things that it is like something to be, as Nagel would put it) and the things that lack it. Even in our own case, we cannot draw the line separating our conscious mental states from our unconscious mental states. The theory of consciousness we have sketched [referring to his book *Consciousness Explained*] allows for many variations of functional architecture, and while the presence of language marks a particularly dramatic increase in imaginative range, versatility, and self-control [...] these powers do not have the *further* power of turning on some special inner light that would otherwise be off.[99]

Also in *Waking Up*, Harris said consciousness is "merely being."[100] If he means merely existing, we are always existing, once conceived, and doing so most of the time without any awareness of ourselves at all. We don't need first-person experiences to merely be. If alive, we be. And finally, after forthrightly declaring consciousness as the only thing that cannot be an illusion,[101] in a discussion regarding pain, Harris wrote, "There is no 'I' that is aware of the pain."[102] I disagree. *Feeling* pain is part of the same illusory sense of subjectivity he calls experience. There cannot be an experience without a descriptive thought or identification of it.

Pain is a hot spot in the study of consciousness. Yet, I maintain there is nothing outstanding about an experience of pain over any other (seeming) experience. Human brains build self-models that (supposedly) experience things, in this case pain.[103] Does that mean we don't feel pain? No. But the word feel is at the heart of the illusion of self and consciousness. We use folk psychological lingo to describe most bodily operations because we don't know the real causes behind them (or it would be cumbersome to reference things in biological terminology). That doesn't mean those are the reasons things occur, or what is actually going on in an organism. The same can be said of pain.

I have compassion that it is the feeling part we're concerned with, but there aren't conscious, feeling selves inside organisms, including us. We just believe it to be so. Reassuringly, consciousness can be a known illusion (not what it seems), and we can nevertheless consider levels of distress to other species in our management of and behavior toward them. It would still be difficult to draw a line between which biological creatures felt pain and which didn't (because what does that mean if there is no person inside the organism?), but this can be approached as an easy problem using scientific measurements.

In conclusion, there is no experiencer of experiences, because there aren't selves in brains to *have* experiences. I recognize Harris also argues against an experiencer—with his assertion that there are no selves—but I find his discussion to imply one. His claim that there is first-person experience (which he calls consciousness) largely aligns with Chalmers' hard problem and defines subjectivity through the lens of Nagel's *what it's like to be a bat* perspective.

We can use the language, "I am experiencing," and realize that sensation is caused by automatic, neurological processes, which are the brain's production of self-models. This is similar to when we use folk-psychological diction in other cases, but know the scientific realities behind them. When commenting, "The Sun is setting," we now understand that that is Earth rotating in relation to the Sun.

Involuntarism

Dennett professed in *Consciousness Explained*:

> How could the brain be the seat of consciousness? [...] I have argued that you can imagine how all that complicated slew of activity in the brain amounts to conscious experience. [...] It turns out that the way to imagine this is to think of the brain as a computer of sorts. The concepts of computer science provide the crutches of imagination we need if we are to stumble across the *terra incognita* between our phenomenology as we know it by "introspection" and our brains as science reveals them to us. By thinking of our brains as information-processing systems, we can gradually dispel the fog and pick our way across the great divide discovering how it might be that our brains produce all the phenomena.[104]

In his work, Frankish promotes a functional conception of consciousness over a phenomenal or qualitative conception of consciousness.

> The alternative is that consciousness consists, not in awareness of private mental qualities, but in a certain relation to the public world—a relation that involves receiving information about things and reacting to them. For one to have a conscious experience

> of something is, I claim, for one to have a rich stream of sense-based information about it and for this information to have a wide range of effects—causing rapid behavioural responses, generating beliefs and desires, evoking memories, triggering associations, initiating emotional responses, and changing one's psychological and behavioural dispositions in a myriad subtle ways.
>
> I am proposing that consciousness is this complex of informational and reactive processes. Similarly, when I talk of us having information about the world, I do not mean that we are something distinct from the brain states that carry the information. These states (scientists often call them representations) are not mental images which need to be observed and interpreted by a soul or self or boss brain system. They are just patterns of neuron firing, which are triggered by the presence of certain features in the environment and have appropriate effects on other brain systems. We are the human organisms partially constituted by these brain systems, and we are aware of the world in virtue of the internal effects these informational states have and the overall psychological and behavioural changes that result.[105]

Thought and awareness present involuntarily. Even the feeling of being conscious is produced by the brain—suddenly, our focus is on something. Being struck with an awareness of any kind is no more voluntary than a blink, heartbeat, sneeze, cough, or stomachache. Even when we are conscious of the wind blowing, for example, that state registers in the form of a message that is spontaneously in our thought process.

Much of this understanding would be to get clear on how we conceive of other functions as being involuntary. How do we think those things happen? What is the source we attribute to cause respiration, circulation, reproduction, immune response, bacterial behavior, digestion, blood cell production, or hormone function? Once acknowledged, we can transfer that comprehension to the workings of the nervous system regarding thinking, perception, memory, feeling, ideas, believing, emotion, learning, attention, decision-making, choosing, intuition, opinion, awareness, meditation, action, experience, subjectivity, and whatever else one may consider the word consciousness to mean. To repeat, brains, as part of nervous systems, have been built by evolution and natural selection. All organisms involuntarily import information and export behavior in ways that are natural to them.

With regard to how something we plan happens, we can look to other creatures. We see planning in the lives of beavers, squirrels, ants, and bees that build and organize incrementally through group cooperation and activity. We are similar, and our use of language is as unique to us as their systems of communication are to them. Though thinking and talking support our needs, they are no more significant, as types of mechanistic contributions, than the apparatuses of other animals to the demands of their lives. With even the most seemingly intricate projects—like sending a Rover to Mars or developing the James Webb Space Telescope, for some examples—there is no extra component, that is *consciousness*, facilitating them. We just have monologues in our heads telling us there are conscious "I's" creating and causing our thinking, communication, planning, decision-making, and action execution.

I have designed a framework I call *Six Guarantees of Involuntarism.* These are observable truths perceivable on the macro level, i.e., without a microscope. Since these conditions account for all human behavior, they are my rationalization for why there is no place or need for a special property called consciousness to produce anything. They mirror Rosenberg's refrain, "The physical facts fix all the facts."[106] On an emotionally supportive level, I offer these physical realities to highlight that we get all these states for free, our whole lives, without having to voluntarily do anything to make them happen. In other words, there is no need to (consciously) exert mentally, or muscularly, the ways it feels. Although these reactions seem intuitive and impossible to avoid, they are illusory in terms of having causal powers (the ways it seems). Thus, letting go—psychologically and muscularly—is always safe.

Existence: This encompasses being alive, with all human systems functioning as they do. The neuromuscular system, being one, is responsible for muscles moving bones at the command of neuronal signaling. This displays our real-time bodily motions that we call actions. As physical organisms, once conceived, we never have to (consciously/voluntarily) do anything to make our bodies be in the spaces they occupy, or move as they do.

Wholeness: A human being is continually a structural, anatomical whole, i.e., parts are physically connected all the time (barring amputations, transplants, and the like). It may seem that the head, or some fictitious inner section (self or soul) comes and goes from the rest of the organism, but that is a delusion. Constant wholeness mandates that a living human always be with the whole of itself.

Gravity: Because of Earth's gravitational pull, we are always on—or otherwise attached to—some surface, such as a piece of furniture, vehicle, floor, or outdoor ground. This status, by nature, indicates action: "I am lying on the ground," "I am sitting on the couch." All bodily movements that take place on the complete collection of surfaces we will ever be on comprise the full extent of everything we will ever do, with nothing left out. (Regarding our attachment to surfaces, I quote myself from Chapter I, Section: "Physical Means Involuntary": "When not obviously sustained by a surface, we float in water or else sink to the bottom, can be suspended in air only with a parachute or cords, and must be attached to ropes and chains when engaging in serious rock climbing.").

Time: The progression of time as we track it—Earth's rotation and revolution around the Sun—transpires outside our (conscious/voluntary) control and provides what we call "next." This natural process inherently displays all our (next) actions automatically. There is no behavior left out of this time-stream.

Thoughts: All mental states—awareness, attention, feelings, emotions, ideas, opinions, beliefs, judgments, intentions, intuitions, and any sense of subjective experience/consciousness—occur involuntarily (on their own). There is no way or need for a human to consciously drum up or choose any type of thought/mental state. We are just in them when and as we are.

All Actions Are Correct: Since we don't have ways of preventing next from emerging—and, thus, our next actions from presenting—what we find ourselves doing in any moment is all that was ever available to us (up until that time). This means all our acts were, are, and will be correct (not morally, but in their occurrences), because there will never be possibilities of different ones. Furthermore, since everything we see ourselves doing is immediately over upon observation, there is no way to go back in time for a redo.

The first five material realities (above) provide a solid base for understanding what I refer to as involuntarism, which cancels out an extra level called consciousness to make us be as we are. The sixth condition is where I land when acknowledging that automatic human functioning, in conjunction with features of our environments, is all we get.

If we had x-ray vision, we would see through each others' exteriors and apprehend ourselves to be purely physical—especially looking through faces to brains with extensions to brain stems, spinal cords, and nerves spreading throughout. Additionally, if we stared at our own skin, we could realize its epidermic quality to be wholly cellular. When an optometrist examines patients' eyes, they see organs, but when we look into each others' eyes, we generally sense something nonphysical (like souls).

Curiously, when looking at insects or shellfish, we don't compute their outsides to be *other than* their biological/chemical insides. Why do our outer surfaces relay impressions of what a human is differently from other species? What is it we see when looking at one another, or in the mirror? In plain sight, we can observe our skeletal structures, limbs moving, skulls included, articulating in their joint connections. Yet we comprehend ourselves and each other through introspective lenses reflecting the (often fictitious) narratives in our minds.

Perceiving our bodies as anything other than indivisibly organized, materially configured systems leads to the massive delusion of a mind-body split, with a characteristic presumption that the mind part has (conscious) control over (the rest of) the body. However, *mind* is not an anatomical word. It references an illusory sense of where an inner self, soul, or conscious entity resides, and where thoughts are housed. But what we are indicating are facets of mushy brain matter, i.e., nerve cells that are as central to the physical organism as is a heart—another word that tends to get *personified.*

CHAPTER IV: Science Versus Story

Evolution

Leading biologist and author, Jerry Coyne, wrote in his book, *Why Evolution Is True*:

> Naturalism is the view that the only way to understand our universe is through the scientific method. Materialism is the idea that the only reality is the physical matter of the universe, and that everything else, including thoughts, will, and emotions, comes from physical laws acting on that matter. The message of evolution, and all of science, is one of naturalistic materialism. Darwinism tells us that, like all species, human beings arose from the working of blind, purposeless forces over eons of time. As far as we can determine, the same forces that gave rise to ferns, mushrooms, lizards, and squirrels also produced us.[107]

He defined evolution:

> In essence, the modern theory of evolution is easy to grasp. It can be summarized in a single (albeit slightly long) sentence: Life on Earth evolved gradually beginning with one primitive species—perhaps a self-replicating molecule—that lived more than 3.5 billion years ago; it then branched out over time, throwing off many new and diverse species; and a mechanism for most (but not all) of evolutionary change is natural selection.[108]

I see my body where it is. This is how I mark my existence and activity as real. For as long as I can see or physically sense my body on the chair, for example, I know I must be in that place (and action). Physical reality mandates a body (of matter) cannot *not* be where it is, or be somewhere it isn't, at any given time. This applies equally when we want a different status for ourselves or other people. Human beings are obliged to be where they are if they are.

Rosenberg talks about our need for storytelling and how science doesn't feel intuitive. I agree; we are drawn to fiction over nonfiction. On personal levels, tuning in to our bodies' momentary whereabouts and movements is not as alluring as our internal movies. Our minds habitually wander into their mental worlds as default modes. There is nothing wrong with this; it is the way we are wired. We can, however, be aware that the messages churning in our thought-trains are often inaccurate reports of how things are or will be.

History of life on Earth is evidenced through bones and other indicators of biological matter—fossils, for example. Where these remnants are found, and their conditions, are what archaeologists and paleontologists base knowledge on about what and how organisms existed. Though we don't typically identify with our bone make-ups, we are able to see that our skeletons occupy spaces all day long, continually giving weight to and interacting with material surfaces and objects. In this regard, we can realize that the nature of our actions is no different than that of past creatures (and others currently among us). We are part of a continuum of organic matter that lives(d) and behaves(d) where and how it does (did).

The placements and gestures of our bones designate the *specificity* of what we do—what we call choices/decisions/actions. We can treat this awareness like a science project. While archaeological discoveries provide legitimacy against mythical records of history (religions, for example), our personal, skeletal positions and whereabouts dictate our behavioral timelines, which disqualifies misinformation delivered by even our own mental commentaries.

One of the coolest aspects of the chain of evolution for me is its gradualness. This ties in with how I like to describe the second-to-second unfoldings of our individual lives. The same way we skip around in our minds when recalling personal events (instead of acknowledging the step-by-step process of each bodily movement bleeding out of the last and into the next), we intellectually exit reality when not grasping that we all descended from the behaviors of ancestral animals like fish, amphibians, reptiles, birds, and other mammals. Since we do not readily capture that our bodies never leave their environments—transforming from one activity into another with the progression of time—it is no surprise how challenging it is to fathom the imperceptibly gradual manner in which evolution and natural selection took, and still take, place.

I adore this thought experiment offered by Dawkins:

> Find a picture of yourself. Now take a picture of your father and place it on top. Then find a picture of his father, your grandfather. Then place on top of that a picture of your grandfather's father, your great-grandfather. [...] And just carry on piling the pictures on top of each other, going back through more and more and more great-great-greats.
>
> How many greats do we need for our thought experiment? Oh, a mere 185 million or so will do nicely!
>
> [...] Believe it or not, your 185-million-greats-grandfather was—a fish. So was your 185-million-greats-grandmother, which is just as well, or they couldn't have mated with each other and you wouldn't be here.
>
> He suggested turning the pile of photographs horizontally, like a bookshelf, and stated:
>
> Each one is like its neighbours in the line, yet if you pick any two pictures far apart in the line they are very different—and if you follow the line from humans back far enough you come to a fish. How can this be?
>
> Actually, it isn't all that difficult to understand. We are quite used to gradual changes that, step by tiny step, one after the other, make up a big change. You

were once a baby. Now you are not.

> [...] And the change happens so gradually that there never is a day when you can say, "This person has suddenly stopped being a baby and become a toddler."[109]

If we adopt Dawkins' experiment and reflect on the sperm and eggs that produced each of our ancestors in our family trees, we land at the beginning of cellular life on Earth. Though this scrutiny may appear tedious, it is basic. Even with ourselves on a macro level, we can observe our organisms on the surfaces they are on—while staring at the clock—to realize our bodily motions (statuses) emerge out of what comes before them, and so on. There are no gaps in physical actions—whether considered on macro or micro levels—because there are no gaps in time.

Why do I harp on about the successive continuity of behavior? Because our mental depictions analyze scenarios in ways that skip in and out of real-time existence, and this come-and-go sensibility fosters illusions of self, free will, and consciousness (the last when considered a voluntary force or power). Essentially, inner narratives falsely relay impressions that things can go otherwise than how they do—physically and incrementally—and that the fictitious we's in our heads can override or avoid determinism.

Regarding human behavior and his argument against free will, Sapolsky commented in his book, *Determined*:

> Why did that moment just occur? "Because of what came before it." Then why did *that* moment just occur? "Because of what came before that," forever, isn't absurd and is, instead, how the universe works. The absurdity amid this seamlessness is to think that we have free will and that it exists because at some point, the state of the world (or of the frontal cortex or neuron or molecule of serotonin [...]) that "came before that" happened out of thin air.[110]

Additionally, the streaming quality of minuscule changes occurring in the histories of all species illustrates how human skillsets evolved from what came before them.[111] As Dawkins brilliantly indicated with his photo-stacking bookshelf analogy, there were never any leaps. Brains/nervous systems before us inched their way into the shapes and operations of our current brain structures in mind-bogglingly slow manners.

This matters with regard to claims of consciousness being other than nervous system functioning.[112] Like Dawkins indicated, there couldn't have been any place in the string of evolution that magically featured one organism's brain fundamentally differently than its immediate predecessor. This also cancels out Descartes' declaration that minds are not material—which influences ways even current scientists get tricked into believing there is something nonphysically mystifying about our mental capacities. Again, there would have never been a temporal opportunity in the engine of evolution for that to have popped in, since "mind" is a shorthand, folk-psychological term for aspects of neurological functioning, and its development was (and continues to be) seamless.

Though Descartes was a highly reputed scientist in his time, his proclamation was a dualistic deduction that went hand-in-hand with other imaginary stories that described human behavior before breakthroughs in neuroscience provided evidence.[113] We can look to other past myths, now known to be mistaken, to appreciate why there will never be anything that won't eventually—in principle—be explainable by science. Some physical processes that used to be fictionally reasoned around the world include: our solar system, fire, life, light, and electricity.[114] The intuitive illusions of selves, free will, and consciousness must be put into that category as well. Even the signaling of neurons was not comprehended until after the discovery of electricity,[115] and now we take that knowledge for granted.

Morality/Moral Responsibility

More from Sapolsky:

> [A]ll we are is the history of our biology, over which we had no control, and of its interaction with environments, over which we also had no control, creating who we are in the moment.[116]

How can we justify that our physical placements and bodily movements (that we see with our naked eyes) are sufficient information to know what we must be doing in our lives—and, thus, what we should be doing? And, that observing them offers greater truths than looking to our ideas, goals, and dreams? This presents the issue of morality because the word should—or shouldn't—is about what we believe to be right and wrong. The practice I have developed, *Mindful Reality*, ties in with ways a number of scientists, psychologists, and naturalist philosophers profess that we do not have free will. They claim all behavior is either determined or undetermined, both excluding the possibility of acting other than how we do. This raises the topic of desert.

Per the *Stanford Encyclopedia of Philosophy:*

> The concept of desert is deeply entrenched in everyday morality. We say that effort deserves success, wrongdoing deserves punishment, innocent suffering deserves sympathy or compensation, virtue deserves happiness, and so on. We think that the getting of what's deserved is just, and that failure to receive what's deserved is unjust. We also believe it's good that a person gets what she deserves, and bad that she doesn't—even if she deserves something bad, like punishment. We assume, too, that it's wrong to treat people better or worse than they deserve, and right to treat them according to their deserts. In these and other ways, the notion of desert pervades our ethical lives.[117]

Philosopher and author Gregg Caruso relayed these words in his TEDx, *The Dark Side of Free Will*:

> I am a free will skeptic. I deny the existence of free

> will. Free will skeptics maintain that who we are and what we do is ultimately the result of factors beyond our control, and because of this, we're never morally responsible for our actions in the basic desert sense, i.e., the sense that would make us truly deserving of praise and blame.[118]

Mindful Reality opens the door to comprehending physical laws on the macro level—the platform where we can view our behaviors without a microscope. We can plainly see our bodies moving in their environments, in real time (including talking and writing), to realize that those actions are the entirety of what we humans do. Furthermore, anything we witness ourselves doing, we must have just done—since by the time we are aware of an event occurring, it has fleetingly become the past. Subsequently, anything we have not done was physically impossible (the full state of the universe being what it is in any given moment).

Behavior flows—our skeletal gestures pouring in and out of each other, leaving no places for us (our mental perceptions of inner selves) to interrupt or impose other actions onto the physical time-streams of our lives. Since those fluid paths of motion consume every millisecond of our existences—with specific activities—there are no breaks for even half-seconds of different acts to materialize (and no outside sources to produce or execute them).

Philosopher Derk Pereboom, who coined the term hard incompatibilism (free will is impossible whether the universe is deterministic or indeterministic),[119] is known for his pronouncement that no free will means no basis for moral responsibility.[120] I agree. For me, being that we can never prevent anything we do—because we only discover our actions upon seeing them already in play—means there is no rationale for just deserts. Thus, moral responsibility holds no ground.

But that doesn't eliminate "core" morality.[121] All species have built-in wirings that cause them to act responsibly as is relevant to their cultures. In this vein, any level of morality humans have ever exhibited was an outcome of deterministic (or indeterministic) causes, put forth by brains (and their interaction with environments). Nothing has changed in the history of humankind, only the understanding of how it happened.

Renowned neurophilosopher, Patricia Churchland, spelled this out in her book, *Touching a Nerve: The Self as Brain*:

> At a deep level, it turns out that moral values, like self-caring values, are in your brain. How did such an evolutionary development come about? The basic answer is that you are a mammal, and mammals have powerful brain networks for extending care beyond self to others: first to offspring, then to mates, then to kin, friends, and even strangers.[122]

There cannot be such a thing as objective morality because no person can consciously control their behavior. Furthermore, much of our sense of what we consider moral stems from religious doctrines. In light of what science tells us about brains, it is useful to reconsider what we mean by concepts of good and evil. Some recommend removing the word morality from our vocabulary because it doesn't make sense—and replacing it with terms like ethics and consequentialism.[123]

Caruso expounded:

> Rather, it is to insist that to hold people truly or ultimately morally responsible for their actions—i.e., to hold them responsible in a non-consequentialist desert-based sense—would be to hold them responsible for the results of the morally arbitrary, for what is ultimately beyond their control, which is fundamentally unfair and unjust. Hence, free will skepticism presents a challenge to retributivism since it does away with the idea of basic desert. If agents do not deserve blame just because they have knowingly done wrong, neither do they deserve punishment just because they have knowingly done wrong.[124]

As addressed in Chapter II: "Crime as Action," if free-willed selves are illusory, how might that alter our emotional, social, and legal responses to disturbing/destructive behaviors? Removal from mainstream society (quarantining) and some types of punishment and accountability remain relevant, but retribution, moral blame, hate, and judgment no longer make sense.[125] This may be comparable to thinking of ourselves as (organic) robots. It is critical to consider brains as biological machinery, which deems them vulnerable and imperfect, like other organs, creatures, and (inorganic) machines.

With no commanding selves guiding brains/nervous systems, as intuited, they are no different than lungs, hearts, livers, or kidneys. With regard to people's actions, we can be smart and sensitive in considering the myriad of possibilities for malfunction and dangerous behavior—not only when those are the results of brain tumors, neurological injuries, or known psychological disorders.

This is the mindset necessary to understand why we ultimately do not need to take human behavior personally in ways we don't with viruses, bacteria, natural disasters, machines, or other animals. We must opt for restorative justice built around cognitive science, neuroscience, education, preventive care, rehabilitation, mental health and social services, addiction treatment, non-discrimination with equal acceptance of all peoples and communities, elimination of poverty and food insecurity, universal healthcare, prevention of domestic and sexual violence, and gun, policing, and carceral reform. The list goes on. Scandinavian countries, especially Norway, are impressively progressive in their criminal justice systems.[126]

Sapolsky imparted:

> Whether at graduation ceremonies you wear the cap and gown or bag the garbage. Whether the thing you are viewed as deserving is a long life of fulfillment or a long prison sentence.
>
> [...] There is no justifiable "deserve." The only possible moral conclusion is that you are no more entitled

to have your needs and desires met than is any other human. That there is no human who is less worthy than you to have their well-being considered. You may think otherwise, because you can't conceive of the threads of causality beneath the surface that made you you, because you have the luxury of deciding that effort and self-discipline aren't made of biology, because you have surrounded yourself with people who think the same. But this is where the science has taken us.[127]

Luck

Understanding we are correct in our actions might make us presume others are wrong, so it is essential to comprehend we are all correct—since anything other than what we each do is physically impossible. If we grasp this, we may experience guilt when acknowledging we are luckier than others, or resentment that we are unluckier. We may be horrified to know none of the offenses committed by the cruelest villains were avoidable (by them), or perplexed to learn the bravest, most altruistic feats by our favorite people were nonconsciously executed. This is difficult to accept because it contradicts our upbringings and belief systems. It is also a good example of how fiction makes more sense to our minds than fact.

Hard-incompatibilism signifies that human lots are determined by physical laws as opposed to deserved, self-caused/earned, character traits. If none of us can freely choose how to act, that means we live in an unfair world—a natural world. We struggle with this conclusion. We long for someone or something to fault other than nature.

Dr. Peter Gill, psychotherapist and educator, articulated:

> A rich capacity for and a generous expression of compassion are hallmarks of good mental health. We believe that compassion stems from a deep conviction that everyone is totally respectworthy and

is "the player of the hand dealt to him." It may be epitomized as "There but for the difference in our determinants go I."

We are part of the animal kingdom. In no essential respect are we qualitatively different from other animals. They, as are we, are totally determined, totally respectworthy, totally innocent in the broad sense, and as are we, they are always doing the best they can at every moment under the circumstances of the moment.[128]

CHAPTER V: The Practice

Mindful Reality

This work is a self-inquiry practice grounded in physical realities that evade our immediate awareness. Our attention is generally on our should-filled thought trains, while our lives in real time can paint substantially different pictures. What we do is what we spend our time doing; not what we think about doing (if they are different). Our proof is that we can witness our activities in real time. This evidence furnishes ammunition against mental judgments that present as, "I should be doing that; I should not be doing this." This practice is a reality check; it is not about justice or morality. It is about coming to terms with the knowledge that what we each do is the truth of what we can do, no matter how unsettling.

Much of the discord between how we believe we should act and what we do wraps around the concept of our next action. This is felt to require mental and/or muscular effort that we presume emanates from a conscious, free, self-backed, decision-making, thought process. It seems we generate next choices of behavior via intentions or what some call consciousness. But there is a catch. Every next second arrives by itself (promptly supplied by Earth's rotations), and within that transaction, our bodies exist solidly in the spaces they occupy, always presenting (to us) in specific next activities *before* we can stop the clock.

It is critical to ascertain that since we cannot prevent next from coming (milliseconds from advancing), we do not have ways to avoid behaviors we do not like. They are incontrovertibly forced upon us (by nature) *because we are always already in them.* This is difficult to fathom if we are continually disappointed with how we act. The good news, however, is that we get all our actions for free, and there is nothing to consciously figure out, despite how it feels. Decisions and choices are biologically executed behind the scenes of awareness, no differently than how our blood circulates without voluntary input.

The opportunity for joy is the effortlessness in *making* our lives happen and the emotional relief that results from surrendering. This aligns with the freedom we get knowing our hearts beat involuntarily, where there is no willfulness required for that function to carry us through life.

Though the lack of conscious contribution may feel frustrating, discouraging, or terrifying, it guarantees we are always doing the right things. Of course, this claim that everyone is correct in their behavior goes against normative thinking. It can thus be lonely living with such awareness and tricky to share with others, because it invites being called crazy or immoral. Even the saying, "We each do the best we can," is skewed since we aren't the choosers of our actions that the word "best" suggests. Although the statement appears to be one of compassion, it still infers dualism—i.e., the presumption one could have acted otherwise—when no such pathway ever existed. It may be more appropriate to say, "We each act the only way we can."

It is strange to feel wrong about how we behave and yet know our actions must be what they are every step of the way. For example, on a light note, it is *correct*—based on physical laws—that (at the time of this writing) I am consuming the abundance of candy I am, even though I *believe* I should not be. This seems odd, since my mental story, that junk food is unhealthy, runs deeply. Regardless, I am watching my hand entering the box repeatedly, and my mouth ingesting the amount of sugar and chocolate that it is.

This scenario would be more troubling if I were diabetic and/or concerned about my weight. Nevertheless, this truth would apply equally to an over-indulgence of cigarettes, drugs, alcohol, sex, spending, gambling, or anything else considered dangerous to one's well-being. Our momentary statuses are always what should be happening because they are the only *physical* possibilities. We discover the specificity of our behaviors precisely at the times we see them in process, at which points it is too late for them to have not come about. And, if we are currently busy in one capacity, it is impossible to simultaneously be doing something else.

Tragically, while not having freedom of alternatives in our

actions, we must still contend with the judgments we—and others—hold about our lives. Since worry, fear, doubt, and self-blame are relentless, this work is never over. Unfortunately, it is the nature of thought to regularly tell us we behave improperly. Additionally, we are preached at from young ages to make certain decisions. But human organisms can export only the acts they do.

This practice is useful when thoughts make us feel guilty, nervous, stressed, regretful, shamed, self-judging, or otherwise pained. Thoughts themselves are harmless; it is believing them that can be mentally disturbing. But our internal screenplays are never based in known truths about how something will unfold. Therefore, it is helpful to be wary of looking to ideas, feelings, beliefs, intuitions, premonitions, opinions, or judgments for guidance, unless that brings you comfort. Since thoughts do not *produce* actions (in a voluntary/conscious manner), we can safely ignore them. Our correct behaviors will occur on time, all the while.

Confronting Worry, Anxiety, and Fear

Actions are always right, even if they don't feel right.

To deal with worry, anxiety, and fear, I notice where my body is and what it is doing. I observe its existence in the space it is occupying as a reminder that this body (called Jill) *must* be here—in this specific activity—right now. Subsequently, if I must be where my body is, I can be assured that that spatial placement and exact activity are my only options of action, for now. This is because: (1) any time I check in with myself, it will be now; (2) whatever I see happening now immediately becomes an event of the past, which means it is too late to retract it; and (3) a body cannot simultaneously be in two places at once, a.k.a., doing something else.

Worry, anxiety, and fear are belief-states that tell us we will (in the future, even if only a second away) be trapped in situations that will overwhelm or destroy us. Accompanying these emotions is an urgent pressure to figure out what to do to avoid those outcomes. To manage these reactions, I acknowledge that all future moments will hold *the same conditions* as the present. My body will be a skeletal whole engaged in a specific physical act, while giving weight to a particular surface in a definite place. And, as with everything up till now, there will not have been a way to have prevented those conditions (because in that present tense of my future, I will only find out what I am doing when seeing myself in the task). Since that place and act will be my only option for that moment, it will have been the right move. If one is alive, these provisions rule.

This means that at all times in the future, we will *know* what to do because our bodies will be in their decisive positions every millisecond of the way. When we realize actions are involuntary/automatic bodily movements, there doesn't need to be any mystery about how to make them happen. We want to feel confident we are making, have made, and will continue to make the right decisions. We are, we have, and we will.

Our familiar convictions that we behave wrongly deems us the bad guys, the incompetent ones. So, either we are all amiss (because we're bad and incompetent), or everyone is always doing the only thing possible. The latter is the truth. We sense there are paths out there for us that aren't our experienced lots, whether it be issues of careers, finances, relationships, appearance, children, health/mental health, immigration status, housing security, or fill in the blank. Regardless, there is no source that holds the key to how we are supposed to survive other than how we exist. The idea that different choices would be more correct is a delusion. The emotional pressure to make better decisions is illogical, since we are all on the right track simply by having been conceived.

When we hope for good luck, that is normal—and sensible—because time continually brings new conditions. We may also fear challenging circumstances, which is natural, but we don't need to worry about how to respond smartly. As incomprehensible (and immoral) as it sounds, there is no way to manage anything inappropriately (in terms of what is *causally* necessary). If internalized, it would be interesting to explore how this last statement could affect people's psychological states. I can honestly say, it has been a miracle of transformation for my attitude toward myself and others.

Final Words—Practicing the Practice

Below is a series of awareness exercises that soothe me. I recommend journaling in the work because it helps counter thought patterns that quickly talk us out of reality. However, if you are able to apply them in your head, that works too. Find ones (or anything I've mentioned in this book) that bring you a release of emotional pressure or pain, and put them up against as many stressful thoughts as you can. Because this is a practice, repetition is key, especially since habitual thinking insidiously persists in trying to unearth our mental ease. Self-inquiry requires diligence and patience, but the rewards are worth it.

All Actions Are Bone Movements

I tell myself my bone movements are the only actions that will ever be available to me, and I cannot choose them. They are all I am allowed to do—but I get them for free. That means no voluntary, effortful decision-making is required. This regards situations concerning money, housing, relationships, children, health, safety, career, work, etc. We think of our lives in stories and pictures in our minds. However, behavior is real-time bodily movement—like a jaw emitting words from a mouth or an index finger tapping a phone. I get a kick out of knowing I could never predict my neuromuscular outputs any more than I can foretell cloud formations outside my window, or the next time I will sneeze. In any of these scenarios, I am grateful when they display activity that makes me feel good.

Watching Involuntarism

All our actions occur automatically in the form of skeletal movements. To practice seeing involuntarism, you can use your breath as a template by observing your ribs going up and down on their own, the way you would witness a cat or dog's body breathing while asleep. Leave yourself alone and notice how your respiration occurs without a will. Then, watch your pulse to discover the same. Take note how these functions are not coming from the *you* intuitively identified with.

Let this familiarize you with other body parts moving (head, torso, arms, legs, hands, feet), including your mouth speaking and finger joints pressing letters on a keyboard. When we acknowledge that all skeletal behavior occurs involuntarily, we can realize the involuntarism of action. Although we presume our bone movements emerge from voluntary pushes of conscious selves/wills—via thoughts and desires—that is an illusion.

Future Outcomes

It helps to separate momentary behavior from suppositions of future outcomes. It's fascinating to note how instantly our thought processes turn *this* action into an assumption of *that* result. But there is no definitive reason to believe this means that. "This" activity only means right now my fingers are texting, foot is on the accelerator, body is in the shower, hands are chopping vegetables, etc. Every physical motion is instantaneously gone, despite a thought that might be attached to it. We can never know what our bodies will do next, or what may result from particular outputs, even if it seems obvious, or we have experienced relatable patterns in the past.

Solving Problems

We are obsessed with mentally solving problems. I take a different approach. I get clear about what action is—my body's status in the space it is occupying—and I make a sentence, "I am writing in the notebook," for example. That is my action right now. Then I tell myself that whatever is on my mind regarding any issue in my life, that current event (writing in the notebook) is the only solution *for that moment.* Since there is no other me to attend to anything, and I am subject to whatever my body is doing, I am always set. You can make as long a list as attacks your mind in terms of things you believe you need to take care of. Then keep making sentences to remind yourself that those are the only answers that will ever be available—in terms of something to do.

How Do I Make It Happen Again?

Something I think causes depression and frustration is when we have memories of things we've done that we liked, and we wish we could do them again. We believe we consciously caused those events and thus become upset when we can't figure out how to reproduce similar conditions. But we didn't cause those acts the first time; life had us in them organically. They were the determined circumstances of that period of time bleeding out of what preceded them. No two moments in life are the same, despite how it feels.

Pleasing the Ego

We like acquisitions. For example, if you wanted a job because it was going to give you money, and then you got the job, you would have the feeling of acquiring the thing you wanted (and, consequently, no longer needing to reach for it). This translates into emotional satisfaction and success, which is a high we live for. So, we can use this practice to achieve the same type of dopamine hit.

When we recognize we are inherently correct in how we spend time, we can consider *that status* an acquisition, since sometimes knowing we are right feels better than getting what we want.

Additionally, we generally experience resolve when knowing we have done all that was physically possible. This is a common thought pattern. I propose we can get the same chemical rush by acknowledging that how we live *is* the pinnacle of possibility because of everything I have stated in this book. We can trick our minds out of their habits of believing something else is the right thing, and know we are guaranteed for life to never make a wrong move. As unintuitive as it sounds, there is no way to miss out on any opportunity. This is challenging, yet powerful. Give the ego what it wants—but change the nature of the treasure.

Successful People

We incessantly compare ourselves to others. Envy and curiosity about how they got to high places consume our inner narratives. We want what they have. I practice noting that those who have mastered outstanding feats were acting involuntarily (nonconsciously) because no one causes their accomplishments. This awareness bypasses our convictions that some people are better than others.

Of course, we value certain behaviors over things that disturb us, however, I feel supported when realizing no individual has innate superpowers that set them apart from the rest of the human race. Unfortunately, nature is unfair. Luck rules, with conditions keeping only a modest proportion healthy, whole, and functioning at admirable levels.

Causally Necessary

I first came upon this term when reading philosophers who were explaining determinism, stating that our behavior is *fully caused* by laws of physics. Because I relate to my organism as an entity of matter, I identify with being caused by molecular laws that drive my body and its actions.

At all times, I am a skeletal structure—my weight falling onto a specific surface because of gravity. If I look out the window or around me when outdoors, I acknowledge I am part of the weather and the rest of nature. It is easy to understand how weather is causally necessary—i.e., its status deterministically proceeding conditions that come before it—since we relate to it as physical. It does itself and feels external to our (assumption of) personal power. I acknowledge my body and its actions are no different.

This phrase—causally necessary—legitimizes my state of

affairs, regardless of how disappointed or fearful I might be in terms of survival. If my current action is *causally* necessary, that buoys my emotional sensibility. It would be comparable to someone believing in a god being told by that deity that everything they had ever done had been necessary, and that they were guaranteed that truth for their future.

This is how I feel knowing I am always on the right track. It also helps me accept that actions around me must be what they are, despite the atrocities. Nature can be cruel, but it is causally necessary.

Endnotes

Cover Page

1 Marvin Minsky, *The Society of Mind* (New York: Simon & Schuster, March 15, 1988), 288.

Some Definitions

2 *The Nature of Free Will: Free Will and Moral Responsibility*, Stanford Encyclopedia of Philosophy (Aug. 21, 2018), plato.stanford.edu/archives/win2019/entries/freewill/#FreeWill-MoraResp.

3 *Free Will*, Britannica (Sept. 25 2025), http://britannica.com/topic/free-will.

4 *Involuntary*, (Sept. 22, 2025), merriam-webster.com.

5 *Automatic*, (Sept 22, 2025), merriam-webster.com.

Opening Statement

6 Sam Harris, *Free Will* (New York: Free Press, 2012), 12.

Chapter I

7 Harris, *Free Will*, 16.

8 Thomas Metzinger, *The Ego Tunnel: The Science of the Mind and the Myth of the Self* (New York: Basic Books, 2009), 37-38.

9 *Preclusion*, Cambridge Dictionary (Sept. 22 2025), http://dictionary.cambridge.org/us/dictionary/english/preclusion.

10 Harris, *Free Will*, 16.

11 Bruce Hood, *The Self Illusion: How the Social Brain Creates Identity* (New York: Oxford University Press, 2012), XI-XIV.

12 Susan Blackmore, *The Self Illusion: Susan Blackmore* (Science and Nonduality, https://youtu.be/Mb_0dCgVnFI?si=TLh-KRIx8FLUw9NMd, 2012), 5:00-6:36.

13 Anil Seth, *Consciousness, Perception, and Controlled Hallucinations with Anil Seth* (Science and Cocktails, https://youtu.be/rcrIv-ztRWE?si=kpdrfYqKWlS70eKK, 2019), 41:25–41:38.

14 Daniel Wegner, *The Illusion of Conscious Will* (Cambridge MA: The MIT Press, 2002), 342.

15 *Folk Psychology as a Theory,* Stanford Encyclopedia of Philosophy (July 1 2021), plato.stanford.edu/entries/folk psychology.

16 Paul M. Churchland, *Matter and Consciousness* (London: The MIT Press, 2013), 73-74.

17 Churchland, *Matter and Consciousness,* 103.

18 Churchland, *Matter and Consciousness,* 81-82.

19 Richard Dawkins, *The Magic of Reality: How We Know What's Really True* (New York: Free Press, September 2012), 18.

Chapter II

20 Michael S. Gazzaniga, *The Mind's Past* (California: Univ. of California Press, 1998), 121.

21 Seth, *Consciousness, Perception, and Controlled Hallucinations with Anil Seth,* 41:25-41:38.

22 Paul Breer, *The Spontaneous Self: Viable Alternatives to Free Will* (USA: Paul Breer, 2012), 79.

23 David Eagleman, *Incognito: The Secret Lives of the Brain* (New York: Vintage Books, 2012),161.

24 Robert M. Sapolsky, *Determined: A Science of Life Without Free Will* (New York: Penguin Books, 2023), 45.

25 Sam Harris, *Waking Up: A Guide to Spirituality Without Religion* (New York: Simon & Schuster, 2014), 101.

26 Gazzaniga, *The Mind's Past,* 19-20.

27 Sapolsky, *Determined: A Science of Life Without Free Will*, 3.

28 Thomas Metzinger, *The Ego Tunnel: The Science of the Mind and the Myth of the Self* (USA: Basic Books, 2009), 37-38.

29 Gazzaniga, *The Mind's Past*, 63-64.

30 Daniel C. Dennett, *Consciousness Explained* (New York: Back Bay Books, 1991), 33.

31 Robert M. Sapolsky, *Behave: The Biology of Humans at our Best and Worst* (New York: Penguin Books, 2017), 587-588.

32 Sam Harris, *The End of Faith* (New York: W. W. Norton & Co., 2014), 12.

33 Harris, *Free Will*, 9.

34 Blackmore: *The Self Illusion: Susan Blackmore*, 5:00–6:36.

35 Bruce Hood, *The Self Illusion: How the Social Brain Creates Identity*, XI-XIV.

36 Harris, *Free Will*, 37, 44.

37 Sapolsky, *Determined: A Science of Life Without Free Will*, 3–4.

38 Daniel Wegner, *The Illusion of Conscious Will* (Cambridge MA: The MIT Press, 2002), 3.

39 Breer, *The Spontaneous Self: Viable Alternatives to Free Will*, 79.

40 Sapolsky, *Determined: A Science of Life Without Free Will*, 301.

41 Sapolsky, *Determined: A Science of Life Without Free Will*, 301.

42 Gregg D. Caruso, *Justice without Retribution: An Epistemic Argument against Retributive Criminal Punishment* (Neuroethics, Vol. 13, No. 1, 2020), 13–28.

43 Free Will skeptic scientists and philosophers: Robert Sapolsky, Sam Harris, David Eagleman, Tom Clark, Gregg Caruso, Alex Rosenberg, Jerry Coyne, Susan Blackmore, Thomas Metzinger, Albert Einstein, Charles Darwin, Richard Dawkins, Stephen Hawking, Daniel Wegner, Galen Strawson.

44 Galen Strawson, *The Impossibility of Moral Responsibility* (Springer: Philosophical Studies, Vol. 75, No. ½, Aug. 1994), 5.

45 Tom Clark, *Fully Caused: Tom Clark* (USA: Ken Batts, 2008), 37.

46 Harris, *Free Will*, 56.

47 Sapolsky, *Determined: A Science of Life Without Free Will*, 34-36.

48 Sapolsky, *Determined: A Science of Life Without Free Will*, 34-36.

49 Sapolsky, *Determined: A Science of Life Without Free Will*, 3.

Chapter III

50 Marvin Minsky and Jeffrey Mishlove, *Mind as Society: Marvin Minsky and Jeffrey Mishlove* (Library of Consciousness, https://www.organism.earth/library/document/mind-as-society).

51 Dennett, *Consciousness Explained*, 173.

52 Susan Blackmore, *Consciousness: A Very Short Introduction* (Oxford: Oxford Univ. Press, 2017), 151.

53 Alex Rosenberg, *The Atheist's Guide to Reality: Enjoying Life without Illusions* (New York: W. W. Norton & Co., 2011), 154.

54 Patricia Churchland, *Touching a Nerve: The Self as Brain* (New York: W. W. Norton & Co., 2013), 176.

55 Churchland, *Matter and Consciousness*, 35.

56 Churchland, *Matter and Consciousness*, 35.

57 Churchland, *Touching a Nerve: The Self as Brain*, 48.

58 Churchland, *Matter and Consciousness*, 12–13.

59 Blackmore, *Consciousness: A Very Short Introduction*, 9.

60 *Qualia*, Stanford Encyclopedia of Philosophy (Aug. 12, 2021), plato.stanford.edu/entries/qualia.

61 Blackmore, *Consciousness: A Very Short Introduction*, 7.

62 Blackmore, *Consciousness: A Very Short Introduction*, 6–9.

63 Blackmore, *Consciousness: A Very Short Introduction*, 8.

64 Blackmore, *Consciousness: A Very Short Introduction*, 8.

65 Blackmore, *Consciousness: A Very Short Introduction*, 6.

66 Blackmore, *Consciousness: A Very Short Introduction*, 6

67 Blackmore, *Consciousness: A Very Short Introduction*, 6.

68 Harris, *Waking Up: A Guide to Spirituality Without Religion*, 51-62.

69 Blackmore, *Consciousness: A Very Short Introduction*, 20-25.

70 Blackmore, *Consciousness: A Very Short Introduction*, 9-10.

71 Blackmore, *Consciousness: A Very Short Introduction*, 132.

72 Blackmore: *The Self Illusion: Susan Blackmore*, 7:40-13:00.

73 Keith Frankish, *Like a Rainbow*, (Keith Frankish Blog, https://www.keithfrankish.com/?s=Like+a+rainbow, May 27, 2022).

74 Rosenberg, *The Atheist's Guide to Reality: Enjoying Life without Illusions*, 233.

75 Blackmore, *Consciousness: A Very Short Introduction*, 14.

76 Blackmore: *The Self Illusion: Susan Blackmore*, 7:40-13:00.

77 Blackmore, *Consciousness: A Very Short Introduction*, 133.

78 Hood, *The Self Illusion: How the Social Brain Creates Identity*, 3.

79 Rosenberg, *The Atheist's Guide to Reality: Enjoying Life without Illusions*, 219.

80 Hood, *The Self Illusion: How the Social Brain Creates Identity*, 3–4.

81 Dennett, *Consciousness Explained*, 279.

82 Edward Maisel, *The Alexander Technique* (USA: Carol Publishing Group, 1995), 75.

83 Michael J. Gelb, *Body Learning: An Introduction to the Alexander Technique* (New York: Henry Holt & Co., 1994), 43-44.

84 Churchland, *Touching a Nerve: The Self as Brain*, 33.

85 Dennett, *Consciousness Explained*, 416.

86 Blackmore, *Consciousness: A Very Short Introduction*, 133.

87 Metzinger, *The Ego Tunnel: The Science of the Mind and the Myth of the Self*, 7.

88 Harris, *Waking Up: A Guide to Spirituality Without Religion*, 53, 57.

89 Harris, *Waking Up: A Guide to Spirituality Without Religion*, 82.

90 Harris, *Waking Up: A Guide to Spirituality Without Religion*, 104.

91 Harris, *Waking Up: A Guide to Spirituality Without Religion*, 62.

92 Rosenberg, *The Atheist's Guide to Reality: Enjoying Life Without Illusions*, 219.

93 Harris, *Waking Up: A Guide to Spirituality Without Religion*,

134.

94 Blackmore, *Consciousness: A Very Short Introduction*, 80.

95 Daniel C. Dennett, *The Magic of Consciousness* (Into the Classroom Media, https://youtu.be/dFTTn-Co5F8?si=3NFk-d5QQ0G-45ZEE, 2016), 39:00-45:00.

96 Harris, *Waking Up: A Guide to Spirituality Without Religion*, 87-88.

97 Metzinger, *The Ego Tunnel: The Science of the Mind and the Myth of the Self*, 1.

98 Harris, *Waking Up: A Guide to Spirituality Without Religion*, 52.

99 Dennett, *Consciousness Explained*, 447.

100 Harris, *Waking Up: A Guide to Spirituality Without Religion*, 91.

101 Harris, *Waking Up: A Guide to Spirituality Without Religion*, 54.

102 Harris, *Waking Up: A Guide to Spirituality Without Religion*, 87.

103 Metzinger, *The Ego Tunnel: The Science of the Mind and the Myth of the Self*, 104-105.

104 Dennett, *Consciousness Explained*, 433.

105 Keith Frankish, *The Demystification of Consciousness* (IAI News: Issue 86, https://iai.tv/articles/the-demystification-of-consciousness-auid-1381, 2020).

106 Rosenberg, *The Atheist's Guide to Reality: Enjoying Life without Illusions*, 20.

Chapter IV

107 Jerry A. Coyne, *Why Evolution Is True* (New York: Viking, 2009), 224.

108 Coyne, *Why Evolution Is True*, 3.

109 Dawkins, *The Magic of Reality: How We Know What's Really True*, 38–42.

110 Sapolsky, *Determined: A Science of Life Without Free Will*, 82-83.

111 Churchland, *Matter and Consciousness*, 191-220.

112 Dennett, *Consciousness Explained*, 37-38.

113 Churchland, *Touching a Nerve: The Self as Brain*, 47.

114 Churchland, *Touching a Nerve: The Self as Brain*, 56-58.

115 Churchland, *Touching a Nerve: The Self as Brain*, 53-54.

116 Sapolsky, *Determined: A Science of Life Without Free Will*, 85.

117 *Desert*, Stanford Encyclopedia of Philosophy (Nov. 12, 2008), plato.stanford.edu/entries/desert.

118 Gregg Caruso, *The Dark Side of Free Will* (TEDx Chemung River, https://youtu.be/rfOMqehl-ZA?si=_mS5aZhMcEVb-ho9B, Nov. 8, 2014), 1:02-1:20.

119 Derk Pereboom, *Living Without Free Will* (Cambridge UK: Cambridge Univ. Press, 2001), xix.

120 Pereboom, *Living Without Free Will*, xviii.

121 Rosenberg, *The Atheist's Guide to Reality: Enjoying Life without Illusions*, 115-117.

122 Churchland, *Touching a Nerve: The Self as Brain*, 86.

123 'Trick Slattery, *Breaking the Free Will Illusion: For the Betterment of Humankind* ('Trick Slattery, 2014), 230.

124 Caruso, *Justice without Retribution: An Epistemic Argument against Retributive Criminal Punishment*, 13-28.

125 Sapolsky, *Determined: A Science of Life Without Free Will*, 5.

126 Sapolsky, *Determined: A Science of Life Without Free Will*, 379-382.

127 Sapolsky, *Determined: A Science of Life Without Free Will*, 402-403.

128 Peter Lawrence Gill, *Fully Caused: Dr. Peter Gill* (USA: Ken Batts, 2008), 49.

Bibliography

BOOKS

Batts, Ken. *Fully Caused: The Benefits of a Naturalistic Understanding of Behavior.* Ken Batts: 2008

Blackmore, Susan. *Consciousness: A Very Short Introduction.* Oxford: Oxford Univ. Press, 2017

Breer, Paul. *The Spontaneous Self: Viable Alternatives to Free Will.* USA: Paul Breer, 2012

Churchland, Patricia. *Touching a Nerve: The Self as Brain.* New York: W. W. Norton & Co., 2013

Churchland, Paul M. *Matter and Consciousness.* Cambridge MA: The MIT Press, 2013

Coyne, Jerry A. *Why Evolution Is True.* New York: Viking, 2009

Dawkins, Richard. *The Magic of Reality: How We Know What's Really True.* New York: Free Press, 2011

Dennett, Daniel C. *Consciousness Explained.* New York: Back Bay Books, 1991

Dennett, Daniel C. *From Bacteria to Bach and Back.* New York: W. W. Norton & Co., 2017

Eagleman, David. *Incognito: The Secret Lives of the Brain.* New York: Vintage Books, 2011

Gazzaniga, Michael S. *The Mind's Past.* California: Univ. of California Press, 1998

Gelb, Michael J. *Body Learning: An Introduction to the Alexander Technique.* New York: Henry Holt & Co., 1994

Graziano, Michael S. A. *Consciousness and the Social Brain.* Oxford: Oxford Univ. Press, 2013

Harris, Sam. *Free Will.* New York: Free Press, 2012

Harris, Sam. *The End of Faith.* New York: W. W. Norton & Co., 2004

Harris, Sam. *Waking Up: A Guide to Spirituality Without Religion.* New York: Simon & Schuster, 2014

Hood, Bruce. *The Self Illusion: How the Social Brain Creates Identity.* Oxford: Oxford Univ. Press, 2012

Metzinger, Thomas. *The Ego Tunnel: The Science of the Mind and the Myth of the Self.* USA: Basic Books, 2009

Pereboom, Derk. *Living Without Free Will.* UK: Cambridge Univ. Press, 2001

Rosenberg, Alex. *The Atheist's Guide to Reality: Enjoying Life Without Illusions.* New York: W. W. Norton & Co., 2011

Ryle, Gilbert. *The Concept of Mind.* Chicago: The Univ. of Chicago Press, 1949

Sapolsky, Robert M. *Behave: The Biology of Humans at Our Best and Worst.* New York: Penguin Books, 2017

Sapolsky, Robert M. *Determined: A Science of Life Without Free Will.* New York: Penguin Books, 2023

Slattery, 'Trick. *Breaking the Free Will Illusion: For the Betterment of Humankind.* USA: 'Trick Slattery, 2014

Stitch, Stephen. *Deconstructing the Mind.* Oxford: Oxford Univ. Press, 1996

Stitch, Stephen. *From Folk Psychology to Cognitive Science: The Case Against Belief.* Cambridge MA: The MIT Press, 1991

Wegner, Daniel M. *The Illusion of Conscious Will:* Cambridge MA: The MIT Press, 2002

VIDEOS

Caruso, Gregg. "The Dark Side of Free Will." *TEDxChemungRiver* (Dec. 9, 2014). https://youtu.be/rfOMqehl-ZA?si=YxgoHN_WClh0tiO-

Dennett, Daniel. "Consciousness Qualia and the 'Hard Problem.'" *Interviewed by Louis Godbout* (Jan. 5 2020). https://youtu.be/eSaEjLZIDqc?si=RQwM6vP9jPxzfs0E

Dennett, Daniel. "The Cartesian Theatre." *The Science Network* (2009). https://youtu.be/a3a2FFoRpzQ?si=Rp8II818a2P5B9lf

Dennett, Daniel. "The Magic of Consciousness." *Into the Classroom Media* (Jan. 9, 2016). https://youtu.be/dFTTn-Co5F8?si=DkiNPyxnpuME2p_D

Dennett, Daniel. "What Is Consciousness?" *Closer to Truth* (Oct. 8, 2020). https://youtu.be/wm8M_xQrgCk?si=r2Mi5FIiWEg0MuJh

Frankish, Keith. "The Illusionist View of Consciousness: Lecture 1: The Illusionist Option." *Moscow Center for Consciousness Studies and Philosophy Faculty of Lomonosov Moscow State Univ.* (March 25, 2021). https://youtu.be/Y2n-s6C1iYQ?si=C2xg0hDxALOB3MzK

Frankish, Keith. "The Illusionist View of Consciousness: Lecture 2: The Case Against Qualia." *Moscow Center for Consciousness Studies and Philosophy Faculty of Lomonosov Moscow State Univ.* (March 25, 2021). https://youtu.be/Lv_q8vTN8ao?si=uLjJH8hzDqibXVPY

Frankish, Keith. "The Illusionist View of Consciousness: Lecture 3: The Case for Illusionism." *Moscow Center for Consciousness Studies and Philosophy Faculty of Lomonosov Moscow State Univ.* (March 25, 2021). https://youtu.be/jXNXewKcDM4?si=KuKZgpdBg3hlrja1

Frankish, Keith. "Why We Can Know What It's Like To Be a Bat and Bats Can't." *Lecture at The Open University Philosophy Department* (Nov. 2, 2022). https://youtu.be/me9WXTx6Z-Q?si=Qoz9GSj-Jh-b3zyt

Frankish Keith. "You Don't Know You're Not a Zombie." *Recorded Discussion With Pete Mandik* (Sept. 2, 2025). https://www.youtube.com/live/k-w04OGJUzE?si=StLYAKYlcOyfF4b4

Blackmore, Susan. "Consciousness, What's the Problem?" *Cheltenham and UK Philosophers* (Sept. 29, 2025). https://youtu.be/T9T1HVAAghU?si=crz6H4OPTx8BGCha

Blackmore, Susan. "Is Consciousness a Thing?" *For the Sake of Argument Podcast* (June 23, 2024). https://youtu.be/Dk4euj7xYOM?si=Gw4WgRmnCCckSGdu

Blackmore, Susan. "Present!—Susan Blackmore: The Self, Free Will and Consciousness." *Mel Van Dusen* (Aug. 9, 2017). https://youtu.be/awED1HYZbsw?si=ugFRity-NN0RFCpN

Blackmore, Susan. "The Self Illusion: Susan Blackmore." *Science and Nonduality Conference* (Sept. 27, 2012). https://youtu.be/Mb_0dCgVnFI?si=a4nhqE3TiueA0uwu

Blackmore, Susan. "What Is It Like?: Susan Blackmore." *Breaking Convention 2025* (Aug. 13, 2025). https://youtu.be/qzUu_EJt3jc?si=-v8vZkFSXChLl_9e

Coyne, Jerry. "Why Evolution Is True." *The Atheist Alliance International Conference sponsored by The Richard Dawkins Foundation for Reason and Science* (Nov. 3, 2009). https://youtu.be/w1m4mATYoig?si=j1yaO3_a-eKX3wp0

Coyne, Jerry. "You Don't Have Free Will." *IMAGINE (INR5): No Religion 5 in Vancouver: Bill J. Castleman* (July 7, 2015). https://youtu.be/Ca7i-D4ddaw?si=BCgIQCyJTdhZHE57

Coyne, Jerry. "You Don't Have Free Will: Question Answer Session." *Science Media Centre, IISER Pune* (Jan. 18, 2018). https://youtu.be/99Erhyrz5EI?si=7gOenSwAALZVcOty

Harris, Sam. "Sam Harris on Free Will." *The Distinguished Science Lecture Series hosted by Michael Shermer and presented by The Skeptics Society in California* (March 25, 2012).

https://youtu.be/pCofmZlC72g?si=1ehEAzpBdUQLQFyw

Minsky, Marvin. "A Society of Minds." *Closer to Truth: Episode 1613 (April 18,* 2020). https://youtu.be/Yz4m65nAM-jg?si=gzk6PQeOcNIiS0Eu

Minsky, Marvin. "What Are Brains?" *Closer to Truth* (Jan. 26, 2016). https://youtu.be/ybUbCgLLRb4?si=ZO8hzVtZUnXZd7iw

Rosenberg, Alex. "Why Are We Here?" *Alex Rosenberg Philosopher.* https://www.whyarewehere.tv/people/alex-rosenberg/

Sapolsky, Robert. "Finding Meaning in a World Without Free Will/Robert Sapolsky." *Into the Magic Shop Podcast* (Nov. 29, 2023). https://youtu.be/md7gD9Mph18?si=f5XIkGD-NYx_Fi_qC

Sapolsky, Robert. "Is There Free Will?: The Unsettling Science Behind Our Everyday Decisions/Dr. Robert Sapolsky." *Finding Mastery* (Oct. 19, 2023). https://youtu.be/iFb4nY-4Bqv8?si=BUPXg7X3GVXV5rwc

Sapolsky, Robert. "Life Without Free Will/ Robert Sapolsky." *The Psychology Podcast* (Oct. 16, 2023). https://youtu.be/iFb-4nY4Bqv8?si=305t9jImLHnlhyta

Sapolsky, Robert. "Robert Sapolsky: Quantum Effects Are Not Free Will." *2/6 Vert Dider* (Dec. 22, 2020). https://youtu.be/m1Ebshc8Ls4?si=5SCRXIFoiRNvgXE8

Sapolsky, Robert. "You Don't Have Free Will: Robert Sapolsky" *1/6 Vert Dider* (Dec. 21, 2020). https://youtu.be/UX7bs4u-vPyc?si=IzYsMhc1-ifOKyn6

Sapolsky, Robert. "You Have No Free Will at All/Dr. Robert Sapolsky." *Big Think* (May 10, 2024). https://youtu.be/ke-8oFS8-fBk?si=1EO3dAPYXGhXJbKG

Seth, Anil. "Consciousness, Perception and Controlled Hallucinations." *Science and Cocktails* (Oct. 29, 2018). https://youtu.be/rcrIv-ztRWE?si=O3DhkO-0vFyPkvcZ

ARTICLES

Caruso, Gregg D. "Justice Without Retribution: An Epistemic Argument Against Criminal Punishment." *Neuroethics* Vol 13 No. 1 (2020), 13–28. https://share.google/2BGnq2dwcFs3Yz2Ar

Frankish, Keith. "Like a Rainbow." *Keith Frankish Blog* (May 27, 2022). https://www.keithfrankish.com/blog/like-a-rainbow/

Frankish, Keith. "The Demystification of Consciousness." *IAI News: Issue 86* (March 20, 2020). https://iai.tv/articles/the-demystification-of-consciousness-auid-1381

Frankish, Keith. "The Lure of the Cartesian Sideshow." *The Philosophers' Magazine* (2024). https://philosophersmag.com/the-lure-of-the-cartesian-sideshow/

Minsky, Marvin and Mishlove, Jeffrey. "Mind as Society." *The Library of Consciousness.* https://www.organism.earth/library/document/mind-as-society

AUDIO

Harris, Sam. "Final Thoughts on Free Will." *Making Sense Podcast: Episode 241* (March 12, 2021). https://www.samharris.org/podcasts/making-sense-episodes/241-final-thoughts-on-free-will

Harris, Sam. "The Light of the Mind: A Conversation with David Chalmers." *Making Sense Podcast: Episode 34* (April 18, 2016). https://www.samharris.org/podcasts/making-sense-episodes/the-light-of-the-mind

www.ingramcontent.com/pod-product-compliance
Lightning Source LLC
Chambersburg PA
CBHW070856280326
41934CB00008B/1468
9798999555250